# GREAT *at* HEART

GARRY HILLS is the President of the Queensland Air Museum, Australia's largest and most diverse aviation collection dedicated to preserving Australia's aviation heritage. After many years as a local church pastoral minister, with a degree in theology, he dedicated himself to the primary care needs of his disabled son, a period in his life which he considers the most consequential. His passion for the preservation of history extends to a profound admiration for Gavin Long, whose quiet, self-effacing dedication is evident in the legacy he gave the Australian people – the 22-volume series *Australia in the War of 1939–1945*.

'Gavin Long was one of Australia's most eminent historians, creating, with others, the 22-volume history of Australia in the Second World War. His extraordinary achievement was largely forgotten until Garry Hills rescued Long's reputation. In this highly readable, moving and generous account of Long's life, Hills has fashioned a tale that all those interested in the story of Australia will want to read.'

**Dr Michael McKernan, Historian**

'Garry Hills has done the right thing by Gavin Long. He succeeds in getting inside Long's ways of thinking and working, showing that he was indeed "great at heart".'

**Professor Peter Stanley, author of *Beyond The Broken Years***

'It is a rare privilege to recommend a book that is both timely and important. *Great at Heart* is both. Gavin Long's legacy has waited too many years for a biography worthy of its significance, but the wait is over. I recommend this fine work to all readers – from professional scholars to all who seek to understand Australia's past. And it's a ripping read to boot!'

**Professor Craig Stockings, Official Historian of Australian Operations in Iraq and Afghanistan, and Australian Peacekeeping Operations in East Timor, UNSW Canberra**

# GREAT *at* HEART

## GAVIN MERRICK LONG
### Australia's official Second World War historian

GARRY HILLS

NEWSOUTH

UNSW Press acknowledges the Bedegal people, the Traditional Owners of the unceded territory on which the Randwick and Kensington campuses of UNSW are situated, and recognises the continuing connection to Country and culture. We pay our respects to Bedegal Elders past and present.

**A NewSouth book**
*Published by*
NewSouth Publishing
University of New South Wales Press Ltd
University of New South Wales
Sydney NSW 2052
AUSTRALIA
https://unsw.press/

Our authorised representative in the EU for product safety is Mare Nostrum Group B.V., Mauritskade 21D, 1091 GC Amsterdam, The Netherlands (gpsr@mare-nostrum.co.uk).


First published 2025

10 9 8 7 6 5 4 3 2 1



NATIONAL LIBRARY OF AUSTRALIA

A catalogue record for this book is available from the National Library of Australia

ISBN: 9781761170201 (paperback)
9781761179242 (ebook)
9781761178412 (ePDF)

*Design* Josephine Pajor-Markus
*Cover design* Luke Causby, Blue Cork
*Cover image* Gavin Merrick Long, General Editor of the Official History, Australia in the War of 1939–45. AWM 043888
Printed and bound by CPI Group (UK) Ltd, Croydon, CR0 4YY



UNSW
SYDNEY

# CONTENT

# FOREWORD

**Peter Stanley**

Australia's official history tradition is venerable and valued. While the first official history was Charles Bean's 15-volume *Official History of Australia in the War of 1914–1918*, it only became a tradition in March 1943 with the appointment of Gavin Long as the official historian of *Australia in the War of 1939–1945*, though it would be another two years before Long would know what his volumes would cover. His series, documenting a longer and more extensive conflict, comprised 22 volumes, more than Bean's, and told a more complex story.

Long shared several attributes with Bean. Coincidentally, both had been born in Bathurst, of clerical families, and both were tall and spare. Curiously, neither ever learned to drive. Like Bean, Long was a newspaperman – he had worked on the *Sydney Morning Herald*, Bean's old paper – but he had surely never contemplated such a massive task. Unlike Bean, he had only ever written stories, despatches and features.

But Long met and discharged his responsibility fully: like Bean's history, it consumed the rest of his life. Indeed, he died in the same year as Bean, 1968, though aged only 67. The authors of his volumes – the largest group of official history writers Australia has ever seen – worked on their volumes largely independently (astonishingly, often part-time, in addition to other demanding jobs). All relied on Long's direction, example and guidance, and formed a notably harmonious team – and Garry Hills shows us why.

While Bean's name is recognised by many Australians with even a passing interest in their country's military history, Long's name is known only to specialists in Australia's Second World War history, and his character is known even less. His unassuming personality, perhaps an asset in getting stories as a journalist, did not make him the story, and to many, he remains only a name on a title page. (Or rather, pages: he wrote three of the Army series of his history and, in his all-too-brief retirement, *MacArthur as Military Commander* and his posthumous

*The Six Years War*.) His modesty, his tragically early death, and the way Australians took their military history for granted for so long, perhaps explain why he did not become a household name.

While Bean has been accorded several substantial biographies, Garry Hills' *Great at Heart* is the first and most welcome biography of Long. Garry Hills has done the right thing by Gavin Long. He traces Long's origins and the educational and newsroom experience that made him the observer and writer he became – the man who Bean selected to be his successor. Garry succeeds in getting inside Long's ways of thinking and working, showing that he was indeed 'great at heart'. As well as restoring to attention an Australian man of letters long denied his due, he also helps us to understand why Long's volumes remain the foundation of research on Australia's Second World War.

We who care about how Australians understand their nation's story are grateful to Garry Hills, and I congratulate him on writing *Great at Heart*.

# INTRODUCTION

'Gavin Long awaits his biographer.'

When I heard these words by Professor Peter Stanley, delivered as part of an address at a UNSW Canberra forum revisiting Charles Bean's legacy in 2016, I was intrigued. Peter sketched what was publicly known about Bean's protégé and successor, Gavin Long, and it was precious little! Yet Long's legacy matches and, in many ways, surpasses that of Bean. He selflessly poured out the best years of his life, facing relentless and complex challenges, to ensure that the world would have a reliable, detailed and accessible account of Australia's participation in the Second World War. Yet to this day, very few people have even heard his name.

I was immediately determined to do what I could to rectify this sad fact and introduce this remarkable man to the world.

It is difficult to say why Gavin Long has never been as well known nor widely acknowledged as his predecessor, Charles Bean. It is particularly puzzling when one considers the vast difference in the public appetite for discussion about the wars in their immediate aftermath. So profoundly devastating was the impact of the Great War on individuals, and so catastrophic as an exercise of international hubris and folly, that the Australian people preferred to put it behind them while they concentrated on picking up the pieces of their lives, praying that it was indeed 'the war to end all wars'. Yet Bean's work did slowly permeate the public consciousness in subsequent decades. By the outbreak of war in 1939, he was relatively well known and respected, not just by students of military history, but also by the public more broadly, and he continues to be acknowledged to this day. By contrast, the national exhaustion after the war of 1939–1945 was accompanied by a general sense that it had been a just, if horrible, exercise – one that a nation could reflect upon with more of a sense of pride and justification. Nazism and fascism had to be defeated and Japanese aggression had to be met. The postwar Australian generation, unlike the post–Great War generation, was determined to rebuild, but was more open to study and acknowledge with pride the nation's participation in the conflict. Despite this, the name of Gavin Long remained known only to military historians.

One might attribute this in part to the different personalities of Bean and Long. Bean was more flamboyant, extroverted and colourful than the quiet, unassuming Long. Also, Long's role as general editor meant that other authors' names appeared on most of the 22-volume series, with his name only on three of them. Perhaps he became the 'tree hidden in the woods', so to speak. As this biography demonstrates, however, Gavin Long was instrumental in the production of every volume, a fact attested to by every author in every preface.

Whatever the reasons, the astounding fact remains that this is Gavin Long's first serious biography.

After the 2016 Canberra forum, I approached Peter Stanley and, with his guidance, began to seek out what could be uncovered about a man whose profound contribution is matched only by his self-effacement. This biography is the result.

A nation, as it matures and develops, does well to look to people who embody its ideals and whose example provides inspiration. The more I have come to know the enigmatic Gavin Long, the more I am convinced that we are poorer for not knowing his name, for not having the opportunity to reflect on his life and work. He introduced Australians to many of our finest sons and daughters who were tested in the crucible of war; yet, the more I came to know him, the more I was convinced that he too was one of our finest.

As a newspaper reporter and then a thoughtful, disciplined historian, Gavin Long masterfully told Australians their own stories. He wore the uniform of an Australian war correspondent in Europe, the Mediterranean and New Guinea and faced mortal danger on more than one occasion to gather and report the stories of Australians at war. He was evacuated from France under German artillery fire and aerial bombardment on the eve of Dunkirk and then again from Greece a year later. But then in 1943, he was tasked by the Commonwealth to oversee the production of an official history of Australia in that global war. For the next 20 years, he dedicated his life to this task. His legacy is a national treasure.

Gavin Long's documents held at the Australian War Memorial provide essential and rich information about his work on *Australia in the War of 1939–1945*. His newspaper reports and published works are available. But the man was self-effacing and this biographer has relied heavily on the Long family's careful preservation of many of Gavin's personal effects – letters, journals, photographs and works of art. Their generosity in sharing these materials, never before seen outside the family, is, in itself, a gift to the nation. Taken together, these documents provide a fascinating, yet incomplete, glimpse into the life and work of this extraordinary Australian – one whose example can inspire us all. It was historian Manning Clark who described Gavin Long as a man 'great at heart' in a letter of condolence he wrote to Gavin's widow, Jocelyn, in 1967. Clark admired Long and declared that Long's style had been an inspiration to him, one that he tried to pass on to his own students of history.

Finally, a note on style. Throughout this book, I refer to the subject by his full name or surname – Gavin Long and Long. I have referred to him by the more personal 'Gavin' when describing personal relationships with family and close friends, and when writing about him as a boy.

# 1
# TO CRYSTALLISE THE FACTS

*… to crystallise the facts once and for all, to establish a story that will carry conviction in other countries and satisfy the men themselves …*

– Gavin Long[1]

Just before dawn on Friday 3 January 1941, Claudie Damm and his brother Bernie huddled side by side in their heavy great coats, balaclavas and leather jerkins against the Libyan desert chill. They waited quietly alongside their mates, primed and ready for the signal to play their part in the Australian Army's first battle of that war – the 6th Division's attack on the Italian coastal fortress town of Bardia.

Claudie Damm was born in Maryborough, Queensland in September 1912. Bernie was born almost exactly five years later. By early 1940, neither had travelled more than 100 kilometres from their birthplace. Claudie, then 27, had a farm at Lagoon Pocket, and Bernie, 22, was a canecutter and timber-getter near Gympie when they decided to head into Maryborough together to volunteer as private soldiers in the Second Australian Imperial Force (AIF). They were assigned service numbers QX3118 and QX3117. Claudie would never return.

On that fateful morning in 1941, the Australians charged into battle burdened by heavy clothing and equipment – rifle, steel helmet, respirator, 150 rounds of ammunition, hand grenades and a 3-day ration of tinned beef and biscuits. The Damm brothers' natural fitness and toughness from farm life and cane cutting had been honed by months of solid Army training. They knew they were in the company of a body of men in fine spirits, many of whom were keenly aware of the reputation their fathers and uncles had earned little more than two decades earlier in the First AIF.

The south-facing Italian defences, less than 400 metres in front of their battalion, were well prepared and on high alert. This was as the Australian commanders expected and wanted – all part of General Iven Mackay's plan to fool the Italians into thinking that this southern section of their 30-kilometre perimeter would be the target of the attackers' main thrust. The plan for that morning was for three companies of the 6th Battalion to stage a 'demonstration' attack in the south – a diversion – while the main attack came against Bardia's weaker western defences. As it transpired, the diversion became a full-throated attack, controversially ordered by the battalion commander, Colonel Arthur Godfrey, resulting in savage and horrible battles over subsequent days that arguably served no good purpose.

The Damm brothers naturally knew nothing of the machinations behind Godfrey's order, but they did know they were going to be attacking a long double line of concrete machine gun posts and sangars along the northern bank of a 'wadi' – a wide, deep, east-west, dry watercourse. To reach these posts, they would have to cross hard, broken ground, scramble 50–70 metres down the steep southern slope of the wadi, cut through the 3-metre-wide barbed wire barrier laid along its trench, then climb back up the northern side, all the while under fire.

Minutes after the attack began, the men in these platoons who successfully crossed the wadi were sheltering in a captured Italian trench that they shared with dead and dying men. They were now under heavy machine gun fire from emplacements beyond the trench and near the centre of Post 11. Sergeant Jo Gullett led three men – Sergeant James Scott and the Damms – in several forays, successfully silencing a number of these machine guns. Scott was killed (as was his brother in the 5th Battalion about 11 kilometres away that same day) and Gullett and Claudie Damm were wounded. They retired to the trench, where Gullett ordered the remaining men back to the Australian line. Claudie had been hit in both legs by this time, so his brother carried him on his back. As they struggled back across open ground, they came under more fire and paused to engage in several skirmishes. Claudie was hit again and killed.

What the Australians did not know until Post 11 surrendered two days later was that their two platoons had been sent in against 350 Italian soldiers who were armed with field guns, mortars, anti-tank guns and 39 machine guns. So disciplined and effective was the barrage they encountered that, of 43 Australians, only four survived.

Fifty-five hours later, the Italian garrison of Bardia surrendered. The 6th Division had suffered 130 killed and 326 wounded. Despite pockets of very effective resistance, the Italians, most of whom had begun the battle in a severely depleted, weakened condition, experienced an ignominious defeat.

Ivor Hele's oil painting of the Battle of Bardia hangs today in the Australian War Memorial (AWM) in Canberra. The painting depicts Australian soldiers fighting and dying in the thick of the attack on Post 11. Yet, in 1966, when he was commissioned to produce the painting, how did Hele know the story of the Damm brothers, who are portrayed in the scene? Jo Gullett's memoir, *Not a Duty Only*, was years away from publication. David Hay's battalion history was almost two decades away. Indeed, how do any of us know the stories of the likes of Claudie and Bernie Damm and the thousands of other Australians who took part in their nation's conflicts?

Claudie and Bernie's story was available to Hele in the same way it is available to anyone who cares to know. There is no need to be a military historian, no need to be related to the Damms or acquainted with their families, no need for any first-hand experience of that conflict or any other.

We know because somebody painstakingly marshalled the facts, collected them into narratives and published them. Naturally, the families of those who have served want and deserve to know the stories of their loved ones; their sons and brothers, their sisters and friends who went to war. But, it is not just the families. If the nation at large does not know what happened, how will that nation honour its fallen and wounded and learn the lessons needed to prevent another generation from enduring more of the same? How poor would that nation be if it had little or no reliable knowledge of its own history?

A person who is tasked to gather the facts of war and weave them into coherent narratives must have the character and capacity to tell the stories truthfully and well – a person with integrity, who will dedicate the necessary years to find out what happened and chronicle the events for all to read. And that person must be given authorisation to consult all available records without fear of censorship, to interview people who were there, to check and verify sources and piece together disparate or disputed details. To know about their nation's role in the war of 1939–1945, Australians have turned primarily to the works of a quiet, unassuming man named Gavin Merrick Long, a man described by Professor Manning Clark as 'great at heart'.[2] Yet very few Australians have heard of him.

Long was described with great affection by long-time friend and colleague, AJ (Bill) Sweeting in the Australian Dictionary of Biography as

> … tall, dark and slender, with hooded brown eyes. He had poor eyesight and looked straight ahead when he walked, conveying an aloofness which was foreign to his nature. In the 1940s he had strong black hair and a close-clipped moustache which contributed to his youthful looks. Although grave and scholarly in appearance, he had a ready wit and a lively sense of humour. He was generous, yet lived austerely. His patched trousers — the repairs only partly concealed beneath a striped, unfashionable, double-breasted coat — and the cold showers which he took until late in life were the products of his upbringing and his aversion to waste. With a preference for simple things, he deplored the passing of the 'horse and buggy' days; he did not like motorcars and did not drive. Shy and sensitive, he recognised those feelings in others.[3]

In 1943, the Australian Government entrusted Gavin Long and his team with the task of telling Australians their own wartime story, in the same way it had entrusted Charles Bean with the task of chronicling the experiences of Australians in the Great War of 1914–18. Gavin Long keenly felt the immense responsibility of the task he had accepted. In an interview with John Hetherington years later, he reflected with characteristic self-deprecation:

> I didn't know when I started how unfitted I was for the job. I went into it with a fairly light heart and great enthusiasm. Because I was Bean's nominee, I thought, if Bean says I can do it, then I can do it. It wasn't long before my temerity began to appal me.[4]

Bean did know his man.

The official history of Australia's involvement in the Second World War is the result of decades of prodigious and painstaking effort by writers, researchers and cartographers, presided over and partly written by Long himself.[5] The history comprises over three million words of text plus maps, charts, photographs and extensive footnotes, bound in 22 volumes, chronicling the people and the events of the war in the air, on land and on sea, abroad and at home. Gavin Long's official history is a national treasure, 'helping Australians to know themselves'.[6]

A so-called 'official history' is a very particular project. For Australia, Charles Bean began what is now a tradition. Gavin Long honoured and built upon Bean's approach, as has every official historian since. But the integrity of official histories has had to be defended, sometimes vigorously in the face of forces that threaten to compromise their essential objectivity and veracity.

In late 2019, Australian newspapers reported that a stoush had developed between the Australian Department of Foreign Affairs and Trade (DFAT) and Australia's current official historian, Professor Craig Stockings, over the publication of his account of the nation's involvement in peacekeeping efforts in East Timor. Stockings, a military historian and former Army officer, was appointed by the Abbott Government in 2015 to lead the team charged with chronicling Australia's military operations in East Timor, Afghanistan and Iraq. He anticipated challenges. 'There are reputations and legacies in play here that may not welcome a robust investigation and publication of the historical record', he said at the time.[7] This was prescient. By late 2019, DFAT officials had, for over a year, been requesting significant alterations to Stockings' draft history – alterations that he found unacceptable. Steadfastly rejecting any attempt at censorship, he said, 'We will include the good and the bad – frictions and mistakes belong to the historical record as much as triumphs. We will write it as we see it, and as the evidence trail indicates'.

Gavin Long, and Charles Bean before him, insisted upon guaranteed freedom from censorship and was formally granted this guarantee by the War Cabinet in December 1945.[8] Stockings is the latest in a line of Australian official historians, each of whom has scrupulously upheld this 'special responsibility'. Since Charles Bean was commissioned to give Australians an accurate and complete – that is, primarily, uncensored – account of their country's involvement in the First World War, there have been five official historians: Gavin Long (Second World War), Professor Robert O'Neill (Korean War), Professor Peter Edwards (Southeast Asian Conflicts after the Second World War), Professor David Horner (Peacekeeping, Humanitarian and Post–Cold War Operations) and Professor Craig Stockings (Iraq, Afghanistan, East Timor). Australia's official history tradition is now a mature, sophisticated and well-respected process; but it is worth recalling how it developed from startlingly humble beginnings.

The citizens of modern, liberal democracies have increasingly come to expect access to credible and trustworthy information and analysis across all of the disciplines, including history. But it was not until the late nineteenth and early twentieth centuries, with the rapid increase in the size and scope of national armies, that democracies saw a parallel growth of popular interest in military history – and not just the flag-waving, 'drums and trumpets' treatments of battles and campaigns. As Gavin Long put it: 'In the 40 years of comparative peace in Europe up until 1854, respect for human life increased, the public was better informed of national and world events, and administrations came under increasing scrutiny. The word "muddle" was beginning to take on its modern meaning'.[9] Faced with the growing horrors of modern technological warfare, an increasingly educated and sophisticated citizenry sought reputable studies of military matters, especially as they related to politics, society, economics and even psychology.

Military histories today are the purview of academic, institutional and even amateur historians. At the very least, these histories 'may act simply as additional flares that help light up the past', but they can be far more than that.[10] In a 1927 London lecture entitled 'On the uses of the study of war', British military historian General Sir Frederick Maurice said that the first 'use' of such study, which most concerns the citizen, is to promote peace by enhancing our understanding of the realities of war. The second 'use', which most concerns the professional, as well as the citizen, is to ensure that war, if it comes, is waged 'in the best possible way'. Hans Delbrück, in the preface to the fourth volume of his monumental *History of the Art of War*, says that he wrote it 'not for the sake of the art of war, but for the sake of world history. If soldiers should read it and find it stimulating, I shall be delighted and honoured; but the book is written for the friends of history by a historian.'[11] Gavin Long clearly embraced this approach. In 1954, he declared that 'one objective of the Australian war histories is frankly a nationalistic one; but side by side with this stands the aim of contributing to the accuracy and balance of history'.[12]

Today, a special subset has developed within the field of military history – the official history. Australia's official histories are commissioned by the Commonwealth government to produce a full, unvarnished account of a specified military operation. Since its inception, the AWM has sponsored the official histories. The histories are official in the sense that they are commissioned by the government as a national record, not in the sense that they present the government's point of view. That would be propaganda, not history. Official histories contain the writers' own informed judgments and interpretations and are meant to provide trustworthy accounts that serve as a point of departure for further research and education. While a team is needed to fulfil such a commission, it has always been the practice to nominate a credible historian to oversee the project, to edit the volumes and also to write some or all of the volumes himself.

It is worth remembering that the writing of official military history in Australia is scarcely more than a century old – Charles Bean's first volume was published in 1920. In 1954, 11 years into his own project, Long gave an address to the Australian and New Zealand Association for the Advancement of Science Conference in Canberra entitled 'The Australian war history tradition'.[13] Long declared that when he took on the monumental task in 1943, he began with Bean, not just because Bean was a mentor, but because Long had no other place to begin. But he went further than Bean. 'I originated little in the technique of writing the war history. I merely followed Bean's principles, modifying these to meet the special requirements of the World War II history.'[14] Because of the wider scope of national participation and more direct role of the Australian Government in the Second World War, Long's history includes volumes dedicated to politics, economics, and science and industry. And as a member of a later generation, Long inevitably brought a new perspective. 'It would be strange,' Long reflected, 'if the confidence and the eager striving of the late Victorian age was not reflected in the work of Bean, et al, and some of the disquietude of the last forty years not reflected in the work of those who have followed them'.[15]

The ground-breaking characteristics of Bean's official history, Long noted, arose partly because of the makeup of the First AIF – a volunteer force, led principally by citizen soldiers, who were 'interested, enterprising and critical' – and partly because of the personality and the approach of Bean himself, a journalist by profession.[16] Bean's personal experiences of the war, for example, led him to mistrust official communiqués and to insist that the instruments of the commanders' will were real human beings whose voices should be heard.

Bean was resolute from the outset that a written undertaking be provided in his contract guaranteeing that the project, including the political volume, would be free from censorship 'as a pledge to returned soldiers and the public'.[17] The effectiveness of this written undertaking was ensured, as Long put it in 1955, because of the strong and well-organised group of returned soldiers whose presence in the background could not be disregarded.

It is noteworthy that, since Long, all of Australia's official historians have been drawn from academia – professional historians, three of whom (O'Neill, Horner and Stockings) had formerly been military officers. Both Long and Bean, by contrast, were newspapermen who had worn the uniforms of war correspondents. This is not surprising, as the most likely place to find trained writers and commentators in Australia up until the 1940s was in newspaper offices. Bean was granted permission by the War Office in London in 1915 to travel with the AIF into battle, and he regarded this as the chance of a lifetime. 'It means,' he said, 'that I shall eventually be able to give the Australian people an account of one of the most interesting events in history *from a position closer than that of any observer* [author's italics] who has been allowed to write his impression of the present war'.[18]

The Australian Government appointed Bean 'official historian' in February 1919. In anticipation, he had begun collecting source materials in 1917. He had in mind a new kind of war history, one that gave the reader a sense of how 'plans made on flagged maps in the General Staff office worked out in actual experience where Billijim and his beloved Lewis gun lay in the mud of a French shell crater'.[19] He collected these materials because he wanted to narrate 'men's endeavour and suffering, anxiety, excitement, disillusionment, stupidity and wisdom'. Gavin Long reflected that Bean sought to 'give a true picture of the test of battle, and to distribute the credit as wisely as possible among those who deserve it'.[20]

Bean applied a journalist's approach to his 12-volume history, finding and verifying evidence by personal experience, observation and note-taking. [21] He filled his own diaries and notebooks with first-hand observations in the field, supplemented with interviews with participants. The experience of the frontline soldier was his focus. For example, in 1919, he visited Gallipoli and later interviewed and corresponded with hundreds of men who had been there to get to the truth of what had happened. In a letter to the defence minister in 1918, he argued that 'Australia has lost thousands of her best and finest men, but I believe that the history of them, and the appeal which their lives will make to young Australians, through galleries and museums, and, not least, the histories of our country, will be the greatest of several great results of their sacrifice'.[22] But Bean had a bigger ambition. Above all else, he wanted his history to be 'true' so those engaged in international relations might heed the lessons of war and avoid another one.

Because Bean lacked expertise in military technicalities – for example, the evolving role of artillery – and because he did not try to draw out lessons for military commanders, some aspects of his history attracted criticism; yet his accounts continue to be useful and reliable. They also offer a penetrating glimpse into Australian society at the time. Bean wrote in the early decades of the newly federated Commonwealth of Australia as it grappled with questions of national identity – a new nation, colonised by Europeans on a continent inhabited for tens of thousands of years by its Indigenous peoples and geographically close to Southeast Asia. For Bean, there were explicit parallels between the emerging national Australian character and the character of the Anzac. He believed that Australian soldiers, sailors, airmen and nurses were 'a fair cross-section of our people' and that the Great War was a crucible in which their mettle was tested.[23]

Bean, as the first Australian official historian, was given freedom to devise and implement a scheme for producing it. His technique grew in part from the nature of his source materials and his need to find the best way to marshal them. He consulted some 21 million foolscap pages of official reports. In addition to this, he had access to more than 300 personal diaries, although he did not use all of them. He also had questionnaires, correspondence, statements of prisoners of war and newspaper files. When assembling the facts of a topic from such a vast array of sources, Bean learned there was no substitute for painstaking thoroughness. He also devised an ingenious system for note-taking, dubbed his 'map method'. Applying this method, he would envisage a blank notebook page as a map, entering, for example, the details of the left flank of a battle on the extreme left of the page and proceeding down in accordance with the sequence of events, helping him clarify the research phase and make sense of vast detail.

Gavin Long was a great admirer of Bean and had closely followed his work for many years. In 1930, Long was in his fourth year as a reporter at the Melbourne *Argus*. Grateful for the employment when 21 per cent of the Australian workforce was unemployed, he found himself nonetheless frustrated by the grinding routine and narrow scope of his professional duties. He had long nursed an ambition to focus his attention and journalistic skills on broader horizons – politics, international affairs, war and peace.

In June of that year, Long wrote to Bean to introduce himself, and, while he did not state it explicitly, the reader gets the sense that he was keen to pave the way for future collaboration. He began by noting that Bean's volumes had given him his most vivid conceptions of the war: 'I wonder if I might say without being presumptuous that I have read the volumes of your history and admire them tremendously'.[24] Long lamented what he perceived as a lack of public interest in the history of Australia's involvement in the Great War: 'I am convinced that an honest and civilised man must be a pacifist and anti-patriotic today. But if the AIF is not enshrined as it deserves to be in our history nothing will be left of it soon but a caricature and a phantom.'

Bean agreed. In a very long reply one week later, he wrote:

> the Australian soldiers were not titans, demigods or supermen, but just Australian citizens, perhaps a little higher-spirited than the average, who in a frightfully severe test proved to have qualities of decision, unselfishness and self-control that most of us would perhaps have not suspected, but which probably exist in ninety out of a hundred Australian boys and girls today. It would be the greatest tragedy, to my mind, if because of all the pompous flatulence of old-time militarism, the younger generation missed the real nobility in the ordinary, unpretentious Australian which – with all his faults – this extreme test showed him to possess.[25]

Bean and Long kept in touch, although they were yet to develop anything approaching a working friendship. By late 1938, now writing columns on defence matters for the *Sydney Morning Herald*, and as war seemed increasingly likely, Long sought Bean's guidance and approval: 'I hope you have read [my articles about defence] and that you think what I have been writing has been sound. I have become increasingly interested in this work since I was first pitchforked into it and have written nothing irresponsibly.'[26]

Long did not really feel he had been 'pitchforked' into writing about defence matters. It was an area he had been keenly interested in for many years and a role where he had demonstrated real talent. His upbringing and temperament forbade him to boast that it had been his quiet ambition for a long time. By now, Bean had been following Long's professional trajectory as a defence writer with interest. So, the following year, when Australia was plunged into yet another world conflict, Long was at the front of his mind when his advice was sought on the need for a new official history.

Bean believed that the war historian in a democracy wields power to inform and guide society's awareness of itself through its understanding of the life and death struggles of its people in war, and ultimately in its shaping of public policy. His passion for an accurate, compelling and lasting history was evident in 1942 when he wrote, reflecting upon his contribution and the challenge that now lay ahead: 'My final hope is that before it is too late (and it is fast becoming so) that there may be definitely selected, with eyes only on capacity and character, the architect who will be responsible for its perhaps greater sequel'.[27] Bean had the very man in mind.

# 2
# MY DEAR LONG

*A son of the Church, he had unfailing integrity and the spiritual stature which reflected the finest aspects of his origins and upbringings.*

– G Hermon Gill[1]

Born in May 1901, Gavin Long's formative years coincided with those of the new Australian Federation. These were years in which British imperial sentiment, 'the crimson thread' of kinship with Britain, was still vivid and strong as the young nation fitfully developed its own sense of itself.[2] While eloquent voices of anti-imperialism were raised – the *Bulletin* published patriotic works by Banjo Paterson, Henry Lawson and Joseph Furphy and decried the 'British Vampire' and 'Union Jackals' – 98 per cent of Australians were of British descent and the largest religious group (41 per cent of religious adherents) was the Church of England. As Gavin Souter put it, 'Nationalism and imperialism beat side by side in many Australian hearts'.[3] Yet, Australia's primary loyalty lay with the British Empire rather than with Britain itself, 'an Empire which comforted Australia against geographical and racial loneliness, and within whose friendly confines the young Commonwealth could feel rather a more important part of the world than in fact it really was'.[4]

The great majority of Australians supported the White Australia Policy, legislated soon after Federation, which codified and exacerbated the oppression of the Indigenous population, denying them citizenship, and looked fearfully towards Asia – a vast region that reinforced the sense of national vulnerability. Charles Bean published his 'Flagships Three' in 1913, in which he articulated the sense of national insecurity at the time:

> The White Australia policy from the first day of its enunciation has of course always depended really on defence … there are matters about which a man worth anything cannot compromise … life which would have to be lived not as you think right but as some Asiatic may think right is not worth living at all.[5]

In primary school, Gavin Long was required to present an essay on the White Australia Policy, the content of which is, sadly, lost; but the fact that this was a topic of study for primary school children demonstrates its currency in the public consciousness of the day.

Public discussions were underway during the early years of the Federation regarding Australia's preparedness for war in the event of an invasion. The Defence Acts of 1903 and 1904 began to legislate the form of an Australian Commonwealth Defence Force, including some form of compulsory military training for all young men, the formation of a standing land force, the division of the continent into military districts and the establishment of a national military training academy. The new Commonwealth had not been won by war or revolution. Bean and others contended that Australia came of age as it endured the baptism of fire of the Great War. Gavin Long came of age along with it. Key influences on him during his early years were his parents, his school and the war.

Gavin was born in the goldmining settlement of Foster in Victoria. He was the firstborn of George and Felicie, known as 'Lexie'. In 1901, the shire of Gippsland numbered fewer than 2000 people, but much activity had come to Foster since a large railway camp had been established there in the 1880s, linking the area to Melbourne. Although the direct influence of the place on Gavin's life was negligible – he was three years old when he and his parents moved from there – it did leave a lasting impression on his parents, especially his father, George, who had a significant influence upon his eldest son. George's lifelong friend, Reverend E Howard Lea, wrote, 'At Foster, the beauty of the bush and its loneliness, the triumphs and the defeats of the settlers, their courage and their perseverance, made an impression on him which he was to carry all his days'.[6] George's work in Foster also illustrates something of his character and ability.

George and Lexie, both Victorian-born, went on to have five more children after Gavin. Lexie was charming, quiet and fond of Charles Dickens and, later, PJ Wodehouse. She was described to the author by her grandson, Jeremy Long, as 'quietly good fun'. Gavin was close to her and often demonstrated echoes of her quiet strength and gentleness. He wrote to her regularly from many far-flung billets throughout his life. Gavin's father, newly ordained and posted to Gippsland, and destined for a bishopric less than a decade later, was the handsome, dutiful and intelligent young Deacon-in-Charge of the Church of England parish in Foster.

George and Lexie arrived in Foster immediately after catastrophic bushfires had devastated the district, razing the recently built church, the vicarage and most of the dwellings. Poverty was widespread. A fine horseman, George frequently crisscrossed the wide district, providing encouragement and material comfort to his parishioners and seeking their support in the rebuilding effort. It was a tough time for all, not least for the families of a dozen of Foster's young men who had gone off to the South African War.

George Long used the considerable force of his personality to rally his parishioners to rebuild their church, only to encounter stubborn, silent resistance. Eventually, at a specially convened gathering, he begged them to explain the reason for their reluctance. He was informed respectfully that a pastor of his gifts was only likely to remain in that parish for a few months before moving on and leaving them to their own devices. On the spot, Long promised to remain in Foster for the next three years if the people would rally. They did, and a successful ministry followed.

While an attentive and thoughtful father, George could display a not-uncommon male reserve in his dealings with his children. This reserve was exacerbated by the expectations of his calling. His letters, written to a teenage Gavin from France and England during the war, while warm and direct, sometimes evinced a habitual formality. He even signed off some of these letters with 'GM Bathurst' or merely

'GM Long, Bishop'. An observer might wonder whether this was over-identification with the role or an oversight by one who was sometimes writing dozens of letters a day in an official capacity and whose formal signature emerged unbidden from muscle memory.

George was ever-ready to state his views to Gavin regarding politics, society and religion, and he maintained his son's respect and admiration. Even though Gavin did not pursue a priestly calling – a blow to his father, which he nonetheless graciously accepted – and church attendance was of very little interest to him throughout his life, there was much of his father's ethics, morality and civic responsibility in him.

Something of George Long's approach to politics and social matters may be gleaned from an address he delivered just a couple of years before Gavin was born. At the age of 23, and in his final year at Trinity College, University of Melbourne, George led his college debating teams in the public constitutional debates held before Federation. In that year, he was also appointed prelector by his peers, which afforded him the honour of delivering a lecture at the annual public meeting of the Trinity College Dialectic Society. That year, the topic was 'The morality of imperialism'. The meeting – minutely reported in the following Saturday newspapers – was held in the Athenaeum Hall on 4 August 1899 and was presided over by the Governor of Victoria, Lord Brassey. The program saw the prelector deliver his address, followed by various eminent speakers. Among these was the Chief Justice of Victoria, Sir John Madden. Lord Brassey added his remarks to conclude the proceedings.

The *Australasian* deemed it a 'racy debate' and the *Argus* printed almost 3000 words providing a blow-by-blow description of the event and the arguments put by each speaker. It provides us a glimpse of the man Gavin Long looked up to during his formative years, and whose outlook he honoured yet grew beyond in his lifetime.

The full text of Long's address has not survived; however, his handwritten synopsis is preserved in the Trinity College archives and the reports of the lecture in the *Argus*, the *Australasian* and the *Advertiser* give us a sense of both the content and the tone of the evening.[7] The lecture and responses were delivered with humour and a good-natured spirit, and the content makes it clear that George Merrick Long, a product of his time and place, was nevertheless an intellect to be reckoned with.

George Long sought to apply 'those axioms of morality commonly regarded as binding between individuals' to relations between states, especially imperial states. He argued that a 'satisfactory' moral case could be made out for Britain's colonisation of Australia. In his synopsis, he wrote: 'What of the Blacks? Was their country stolen? No! Possession is only applicable to an organised community. Rights begin with the State; the Blacks had no State.' He continued: 'Condemnation may fall on our actual dealings with the aborigines, but not on the principle of occupation'.

His four-point summary of the moral considerations that apply to any nation 'aspiring to imperial possessions' is typical of the waning British liberal imperialism and waxing liberal reformism of the day: that colonies may be planted where no 'real government' already exists, providing due consideration is given to any aboriginal peoples; that she may not invade an established government 'for material considerations only'; that if a government has been disrupted in the past, the coloniser should 'seek to retire them again in due time and manner'; and that she may intervene temporarily in 'a disordered State in the interests of humanity'. Long was not arguing for the end of empire but foreshadowing, 'on moral grounds', today's Commonwealth.

The Longs left Foster in 1904 when George accepted appointment as founding headmaster at Trinity Grammar School, Kew, and it was there that Gavin began his formal schooling. George accepted the post despite the possibility of more lucrative and prestigious posts soon to be on offer, and it was the first of several he would accept with a distinct emphasis on education. He was offered numerous prestigious parish appointments in Melbourne but consistently refused them.

We can only guess the effect on a young Gavin, attending a small school in which he was known to all as the eldest son of the headmaster. Fortunately for him, that headmaster seems to have been widely respected and admired. Trinity grew under his headmastership from a few dozen to 300 boys, in no small part because of George's reputation. One of the students he encouraged, Martin Boyd, went on to base the character of 'The Mugger' in his novel *The Montforts* on George Long. One father who sent several of his sons to Trinity held Long in such high regard he wrote of Long's headmastership:

> I sent my boys to [Trinity] at considerable inconvenience and in preference to nearer schools. [Long] had a mysterious gift of personality which excites the personal devotion and enthusiasm of the boys. He had dignity without stiffness, and a very approachable friendliness of manner without familiarity. He had a power of inspiring the boys with a hatred of everything mean and insincere. I had a profound respect for the sincerity of his convictions, his broadminded tolerance, and his real spirituality.[8]

George Long's biographer, William Johnson, Anglican Dean of Newcastle when Long was Bishop there, asserts that George was 'dismayed' when unanimously elected Bishop of Bathurst in 1911: 'He sought out his wife and handing her the telegram, sat on the kitchen table dangling his legs, and looking the picture of complete dejection. He was thirty-six.'[9] Johnson admiringly declares that Long had intended to spend his life in educational work; however, his superiors urged it was his duty to accept the demanding challenge of the bishopric. This duty he accepted. For Gavin Long, this meant relocating with his family to Bathurst and All Saints' College.

All Saints' College was established in 1874 as the Bathurst Church of England College with just seven students. Charles Bean's father Edwin had been headmaster there for 11 years until 1889. By the time the Long family moved to Bathurst in 1911, the College was under the headmastership of George Stiles, who had just taken over from HE Britten, the father of Gavin's future wife, Jocelyn. When Long began, there were 29 boarding students and 11 'day boys'. He rode to school daily on a pony. Between 1913 and 1918, enrolments totalled between 45 and 50 boys each year. As at Trinity Grammar, Gavin participated in a small student body with a celebrated father – the bishop, no less.

In such circumstances, some sons might rebel; but he showed no signs of rebellion. He was, in fact, a model student.

The school was an antipodean version of many a public school in England. Something of the ethos at All Saints' at that time can be gleaned from the reflections of an Old Boy, Norman Wallis, who was there at the same time as Gavin.[10] Wallis notes that everyone had a nickname: 'Ham', 'Algy', 'Chook', 'Peggy', 'Rubber'. He recalled that 'By 1917, we were a small, happy, mischievous crowd, with dormitories raiding one another after lights out, Saturday evening debates and boxing contests.' When they received the news of Old Boy Alan Blacket's death, the rugby team responded by ensuring that there could be no thought of the team letting the school down. Blacket had enlisted in 1915 and was a second lieutenant in the 19th Infantry Battalion when he was killed in August 1918. Indeed, the connection with those engaged in the far-away war was an emotional one. Wallis continued: 'Most of us will look back with a good deal of feeling to the Chapel evenings. The war period was one of great stress. Canon Wilton spoke to us as boys who would soon be men.' The students 'played war' with one another, with studies (student alcoves) serving as positions against which to fight other studies: 'One can see the holes driven through the mortar, or where an old brick had been removed so that bungers or "jumping jacks" (fireworks) could be introduced through these "saps" to the "enemy".' Wallis cites the school motto as *Vim promovemus insitam* (We develop the inner strength). In fact, the full motto was *Deo Auctore Vim Promovemus Insitam* (With God as our guide, we develop the inner strength).

One is left to imagine today how the minds of young men were being shaped in a Church of England school in provincial New South Wales during the Great War. The junior Army cadets at All Saints', established in 1907, had been disbanded in 1911 after the Australian Government, following the advice of Lord Kitchener, introduced universal compulsory service for eligible boys aged between 12 and 26. In 1914, the catastrophe of war in Europe had reached all corners of the British Empire. All Saints' College in Bathurst was no exception. News would all too often reach the school about Old Boys who had been killed or wounded in action. Between 1915 and 1918, over 200 Old Boys and College staff served with British and Australian forces, most of them with the AIF. Thirty-four Old Boys were killed in action or died of wounds. Thirty-three gained decorations, including one Victoria Cross. Of the casualties, four were Long's contemporaries. There is no evidence that Gavin was enthusiastically 'warlike' – when he became eligible to enlist, he did not volunteer – but he and his school chums avidly read whatever war news they could get their hands on, pouring over battle maps and sketches published in the *Illustrated London News* and the *Sydney Mail*.

Throughout 1917 and 1918, Gavin corresponded regularly with two men serving with the AIF in Europe – his father and one of his teachers, William Richard 'Gus' Brown. Brown, who was popular with the boys, had resigned his post as the school's Mathematics and Latin Master to enlist. According to All Saints' historians, Brown 'employed methodical, boy-proof teaching methods' and was 'a quiet, sympathetic influence in and out of the classroom'.[11] All Saints' Old Boy Norman Wallis reflected in 1937, 'We all feared "Gus" Brown, but we respected and admired him more'. On 7 February 1917, Brown had embarked for the Western Front with the 24th batch of reinforcements of the 13th Infantry Battalion. Brown served as a lieutenant, initially with the 7th Machine Gun Company and then with the 2nd Machine Gun Battalion in Belgium and France.

Towards the end of April 1917, Gavin received a letter from Brown, addressed 'My dear Long', in reply to one he had sent informing his teacher that he had passed his Intermediate exams.[12] Long received a B for English, History, Geography and Maths, and we can imagine he was especially pleased to report an A in Latin. Brown was clearly a conscientious and kind master, respected and appreciated by his students, especially Long. He congratulated him on his A in Latin, writing: 'I'm sure now you will not regret those wearisome hours you put in with me. You all worked very hard, and if you owe anything to me, I also owe thanks to all of you for making my work easy and a pleasure.'

Gavin wrote to him again in September of that year with news of his progress and the life of the school in general. He received a reply in November, addressed from France, thanking him for remaining in contact, as not all the boys had done this. One can imagine the impact on the impressionable mind of the young boy in Bathurst corresponding regularly with his father and with a respected teacher, both of whom were immersed in far-off battles in Europe.

In an otherwise unremarkable letter to his young student, comprising questions about the doings at All Saints' and the local weather, Brown recalled poignantly his experiences in the Belgian line. 'The desolation is heartbreaking and one could not conceive anything like the ruin of that city which has been the scene of so much bitter fighting for three years.' Brown's letter provided a vivid narrative of his experiences in battle: 'We had a thrilling time getting out from the enemy's shells. Fritz launched a severe gas-shell attack while we were in but the respirators are a marvellous protection. It is Phosgene that he uses now mostly.'

In April 1918, Brown wrote from France once again, thanking Gavin for continuing to stay in touch, noting that the boy's February letter reached him 'in the line'. Brown reported in brisk prose that the 'artillery is very active on both sides all the time, and our positions come in for plenty of shelling'. Machine gun units, armed with Vickers tripod-mounted machine guns, were often deployed in exposed positions, in support of infantry, and suffered heavy casualties. Gus Brown, however, lived to see the end of the horrors of those years and returned to Australia in June 1919, joining the staff at The King's School, Parramatta, where he served as Master of Macarthur House.

Gavin also corresponded every month or so with his father, who had been commissioned as an Army chaplain in December 1917 and whose signal contribution to the war effort was his oversight of the Australian Imperial Forces Educational Service, the brainchild of the Chief of Staff, General Brudenell-White.[13] The scheme provided vocational training to servicemen to prepare them for a return to civilian life in a trade or industry, agriculture, commerce or business. Unfortunately, it was set up too late to be fully ready by the time of the Armistice, but did provide some training for over 100 000 men during the long AIF demobilisation. Charles Bean called Bishop Long 'one of the great Australians of his generation', whose contribution to the 'turning of the AIF's effort from destruction to construction may well be judged Long's greatest work'. Even though the scheme did not achieve all that was hoped, Bean asserted that 'no part of the AIF's war effort so richly repaid the nation, turning men's thoughts to their own and the nation's future'.[14]

While in France and England, George wrote lengthy, longhand letters to his son, with interesting descriptions of the countryside, local customs and the daily doings of a chaplain, variously signing his letters 'yours with love', 'dad', 'your loving father' and, as noted earlier, 'GM Bathurst' or 'GM Long, Bishop'. He described conducting religious services, visiting casualty clearing stations and laying the groundwork for the educational work. He dismissively described the 'dastardly Boche' who dropped bombs from the air. In April 1918, from an Australian reinforcement camp, he was impressed by the spirit of the Australian soldiers he met, optimistically writing: 'No-one doubts that the Australians will hold the line. There is no doubt the Aussies are very confident about themselves and there is no doubt they are great troops. They have never failed. The old pukka British army admires them greatly, especially the Scotch.'[15] One cannot know whether George's ebullient descriptions of the Australian soldier in these personal letters arose from genuine admiration gleaned from first-hand experience, or whether they were, at least in part, meant to alleviate the fears of his family so far away. In years to come, Gavin Long's writings would generally evince a sanguine, if less ebullient, attitude toward the Australian soldier.

In May 1918, displaying the kind of gentle humour that often coloured Gavin's later writings as a reporter and essayist, George related an incident in which a British colonel had expressed amazement that an Australian private at Amiens had saluted him. He joked to his son that he had advised the colonel to enter the date in his diary and to celebrate it year by year. He rounded out the anecdote with a typical example of rousing commentary about Australian soldiers: 'They don't know how to salute and they don't know how to surrender'.[16]

Gavin Long respectfully followed his father's advice regarding study and work. In January 1919, George advised: 'When you do go [to university], just take things quietly and sensibly and do your work steadily. Take up a reasonable number of College interests. I know games bore you rather but everyone ought to be something of a master of at least one game.'[17] Gavin took up rowing at college and loved it, and he proceeded, as advised, 'patiently and quietly in College, taking things coolly'.

That January, George received the honorary rank of Brigadier and was awarded a CBE (Commander of the Order of the British Empire). By March, after months of his typically rigorous and energetic application of himself to his duties, his health had begun to break down and he made plans to return to Australia. He arrived home in July 1919, as reported in the *Advocate*, 'to a large crowd of Bathurstians who turned out to cheer him at the station' and, despite weariness and poor health, immediately returned to a vigorous ministry in Bathurst.

It was also during these formative years at All Saints' that Gavin began to be acquainted, if indirectly, with another Old Boy, Charles Bean. Bean was born at Bathurst in 1879 and attended All Saints' when his father, Edwin, was the principal. During the war, Long 'read every scrap of war news', no doubt reading some of Bean's despatches as the official war correspondent.

Bean was a reporter with the *Sydney Morning Herald*, and its London correspondent between 1911 and 1913, before being commissioned as the Commonwealth's official war correspondent and then official historian. Long had moved from Bathurst to Sydney by the time he read the announcement of Bean's appointment as historian in the *Sydney Morning Herald* in May 1919:

> Mr. Bean will now devote himself to the historical record of Australia's part in the world's re-birth, a task he is peculiarly fitted to fulfil. He has had personal touch with every field in which Australia has been engaged in Gallipoli and France, a privilege enjoyed by no other soldier or writer. His information, gained at first hand, will, therefore, be of vast historical importance.[18]

Bean's career was mirrored by Long a few decades later in all respects but one – that of Australia's official war correspondent. Long was considered for that role in 1940, but it was offered instead to Kenneth Slessor. Bean's influence upon Gavin Long cannot be overstated.

Gavin did well academically at All Saints' College. He was dux of the school in 1917. And in November 1918, aged 17, he completed his Leaving Certificate. The exam, scheduled for 11 November, was postponed for a day because of the Armistice. It must have been hard to concentrate on maths formulae and Latin verbs when so much of the world was celebrating the official end to the war. Despite this, Long achieved Second-Class Honours, with a Pass in Latin, Greek, Mathematics and Modern History, and a High Pass in English.

He enrolled in an Arts degree at the University of Sydney and moved into St Paul's College at a time when the after-effects of the war were keenly felt. Many years later, in conversation with journalist, author and war correspondent John Hetherington, he recalled: 'When I reached the university, about half the residents of every college were young returned soldiers who had seen hard fighting. The rest of us looked up to them. We felt we lacked something they had. We belonged to a lesser breed.'[19]

As an Old Boy of All Saints', Long was a member of an intimate Bathurstian Anglican circle in Sydney. Between 1922 and 1925, three former All Saints' masters, including Gus Brown and two Old Boys, including Long, joined the staff at The King's College, Parramatta, where Herbert Britten, a past All Saints' headmaster, was already on staff at Macarthur House. Long was appointed Assistant Master of Thomas House in 1922. That year, he coached the successful 'four' from King's in the Great Public Schools rowing competition, the only sport in which he ever really showed an interest.

In 1924, still unclear about a career, he took up a Diploma of Education. On 10 January 1925, after completing the diploma and briefly holidaying at his parents' home in Bathurst, Long boarded the Commonwealth-owned steamer *Largs Bay* to sail from Sydney to Plymouth via the Suez Canal. He expected to be away for at least

12 months. Eschewing a teaching role, he quickly secured work in the Migration and Settlement Office at Australia House, interviewing prospective immigrants. One of the attractions, perhaps the main attraction of this sabbatical, was the presence of 21-year-old Jocelyn 'Jocie' Britten, eldest daughter of Herbert and Mary Britten, who was holidaying there with her grandmother. Gavin had been tentatively courting Jocie for some months, and family tradition has it that, when he fetched up at Jocelyn's aunt's place in Cornwall where she was staying, tall and gaunt in a threadbare overcoat in a snowstorm, he made a lasting impression.

Unlike Gavin, Jocelyn was a socialite. She was lively, outgoing and very clear about who she liked and didn't like. She was extroverted, talkative and energetic, with little regard for the strictures of the accepted 'woman's role' of that era. She had a driver's licence, unlike Gavin, who had little interest in modern contrivances like motor cars, preferring to walk or take a bus or train. Throughout their married life, she did the driving. In Cornwall, they swam, walked in the country and planned a future together. On 5 September 1925, vexed that Jocie was soon to return to Australia – Gavin did not return until the following March – they were secretly married at the registry office in Kensington. The new Mrs Long sailed two weeks later as Gavin travelled to Europe with an old Bathurst chum for something of a bachelor's honeymoon.

By the time he returned to Australia six months later, Long had gained some clarity about a chosen profession, and in June 1926, he eagerly accepted a position as a 'junior' at the Melbourne *Argus.* His career as a newspaperman and his lifelong craft as a wordsmith had begun.

# 3
# NEWSPAPERMAN, ARTS CRITIC AND DEFENCE COMMENTATOR

*Long was an excellent journalist.*

– Gavin Souter[1]

Gavin Long's interest in journalism was stimulated by contributions he made to newspapers and journals during his university days and while on sabbatical in London. After choosing to pursue a Bachelor of Arts and a Diploma of Education rather than following his father into the Anglican ministry, he briefly experimented with another course correction in 1924 – he became a reporter for the small, newly established newspaper, *The Daily Guardian*, published in Sydney between 1923 and 1931. A general reporter's job in 1924 paid 5 pounds a week, close to the average wage for male workers at that time.

In June 1926, when he accepted a position as a 'junior' at the *Argus* in Melbourne, his father wrote, in typically encouraging fashion, 'I am glad you have decided to go with the Argus. It is, I believe, the best service in the Commonwealth'.[2] He went on to opine at length that, while the 'point of view' of the paper was a little too politically and socially conservative for his liking, 'they are decent to their staff'. His father was referring to the fact that the *Argus*, as distinct from *The Age*, was regarded as the conservative voice of the financial, trading, import-export and grazing industries. The paper was held in high esteem as a training ground for journalists, pairing cadet journalists with senior journalists or assigning 'rounds', such as crime, local politics, courts, defence, shipping, etc. Long was particularly taken with the *Argus*'s weekend magazine, which made use of a new colour-printing technique.

A story appeared in the 10 May edition of the *Argus* in 1927 that illustrated the primitive nature of Australian journalism at that time and the lengths that journalists and editors sometimes went to in order to publish a story. When the paper wanted to publish next-day photos of the opening of Parliament House in Canberra, the journalist, carrying a parcel of negatives, had to travel 500 kilometres in a de Havilland biplane, ride a horse-drawn jinker, drive a hire car over bad roads and a damaged bridge, and take a special one-car train through the dark from Wangaratta. Once they got to Melbourne station at 9:30 pm, they were met by newspaper staff who immediately spirited the negatives away to be developed, set and printed in time for the morning edition.

It became clear from the outset that Gavin Long had the makings of an enterprising and versatile newspaperman. He had a capacity for accurate and objective reporting as well as a flair for lively, readable copy. He was that rare combination of a good reporter and a good writer – not necessarily the same thing. He was now receiving 6 pounds, 12 shillings and 6 pence a week, and quipped years later: 'After I had been in Melbourne a few weeks this six pounds twelve and six went to my head and I got married'.[3] While he and Jocelyn had already secretly married, it was now publicly solemnised at St Peter's Anglican Church, Eastern Hill, Melbourne. The new Mr and Mrs Long had 160 pounds in the bank and they were the proud owners of a new Baby Austin car, a gift from Jocie's parents. With Gavin's modest income, they initially took up residence in a flat in the Queen's Palace building in Carlton – a 'musty old building full of statuary' –boasting three unfurnished rooms, with shared use of a bathroom.[4] It wasn't until late the following year that the Longs, now enjoying a sub-editor's salary, felt sufficiently confident to purchase a house in Middle Brighton for 1575 pounds, with a 1000-pound mortgage and a loan from the Long seniors.

The *Argus* promoted Long, first to senior reporter, then sub-editor. Throughout 1930 and 1931, in addition to his regular reporting, Long wrote witty, erudite and entertaining sketch pieces for the Saturday edition, which provide a glimpse into the lively, wide-ranging activity of his mind. For example, under the title 'Notable nobodies', he detailed the origins of such vernacular terms as 'Uncle Sam', 'John Doe' and 'before you can say Jack Robinson'. In a piece entitled 'A century of abuse', he traced the amusingly idiosyncratic, symbiotic relationship between artists and their critics. He even produced for the reader a detailed, international history of snow skiing!

The following opening paragraphs are from a piece that appeared on 27 September 1930 under the heading 'Record-breaking in the fifties: Prodigious feats of the Flying Pieman' in which Long described the mid-nineteenth-century exploits of William Francis King, an eccentric character, the so-called 'Pieman', who made a name for himself performing all manner of outlandish stunts until he 'died, forgotten, at an asylum in Liverpool (NSW) in 1874'. The excerpt is a good example of Long's zesty, highly entertaining writing style:

> At 3pm on September 12, a citizen of Melbourne arrived naked and exhausted at the Moreton (W.A.) telegraph station, having walked 140 lonely miles since August 28; at 10am next morning Doyiah Chapuelow left the general post office at Sydney to walk to Perth; an hour later a girl collapsed at Townsville (Q.) after having danced continuously for 95 hours – a world's record, it is said, for a woman dancer. Record-breaking is endemic. No one can be certain that tomorrow an enthusiast in Moose Neck (Da.) will not begin an attempt to cat 100 hard-boiled eggs in 100 minutes, or that a playful Parisian will not undertake to carry a grand piano to the top of the Eiffel Tower.
>
> There was a notable outbreak of this kind of thing in Australia in the 'forties and spacious 'fifties. The un-athletic 18th century had passed; lily-white amateurism and the revival of the Olympiad had not arrived. Contests were informal and picturesque. The giants of those days sometimes walked or ran their distances; more often they walked backward, wheeled a hand-cart or coach, leaped or crawled. These contests generally began and ended at a hotel, where the competitors could find backers, an appreciative audience, and someone to hold the stakes and their cravats and hats.[5]

During his teaching days in Sydney, Long developed an interest in film and theatre criticism, and while in London during 1925, he sent theatre notes and some verse to the Sydney magazine, *The Triad*, a journal devoted to literary, pictorial, musical and dramatic art, published to a wide readership in Australia, New Zealand and beyond between 1915 and 1927. *The Triad* provided a platform for would-be novelists, poets and literary critics. Long sent some verse, which was never published – at least, not under his own name; it is conceivable that he used a pseudonym – as well as a couple of contributions under the title 'Some London theatres'. *The Triad* stated: 'The young Australian who wrote these illuminating notes was asked by *The Triad* to keep an eye on things theatrical in London'.[6] This was quite a feather in his cap at the age of 26. The magazine placed a high value on erudite theatre reporting and criticism, featuring regular Sydney and Melbourne theatre notes.

From June 1927, he supplemented his modest income at the *Argus* by writing a weekly review of films for *The Australasian* magazine. In an obituary in 1968, *Canberra Times* reporter Robert Moss claimed that the film reviews Long wrote in the late 1920s were an early attempt to give serious attention to a still novel medium. Moss claimed that at the *Argus*, Long conducted the first film reviewing ever attempted in Australia. However, Moss gives Long too much credit. Film reviewing in Australia dates back to the first public viewings in October 1896, with reviews appearing in a number of mainstream daily newspapers. Both general and specialist media outlets reviewed films. By the 1920s, a large number of film journals, magazines, fan newsletters and trade papers published film reviews, including *Smith's Weekly* between 1927 and 1940, in which Kenneth Slessor's reviews and essays on film culture and production appeared under the heading 'Through Smith's private projector'.

In the extensive index of the definitive *A Companion to the Australian Media* published in 2014, there is no mention of Gavin Long, nor is he mentioned in Ron Perlgut's article 'Film reviewing in Australia' in the same volume.[7] One is led to conclude that Gavin Long, the film reviewer, has never been held in sufficiently high regard by those acquainted with the field. On the other hand, as it has taken more than 50 years for a biography of Long to emerge, perhaps this is yet another example of Long's uncanny ability to glide wraith-like through history, all the while making a significant, if unsung, contribution.

In 1932, he began writing a weekly page on films for the *Sydney Mail* under the heading 'At the pictures – Latest talkies reviewed'. He clearly maintained an abiding interest. He contributed about 45 articles in 1935, reviewing 145 films that year alone. That is three to four films per week! One may conclude that he was on first-name terms with picture show owners in Sydney. On 17 April that year, he devoted an entire page to one film – Chauvel's award-winning *Heritage*, released that week. He was a passionate advocate for the nascent Australian film industry. His film reviews are lively and well written, revealing a broad knowledge of literature and an appreciation for the art and science of motion picture production. He soon branched into theatre, music and art criticism for the Melbourne *Herald*.

In the same year, Long revealed an impressive knowledge of art in an essay he wrote entitled 'A layman's complaint', which was published in the pioneering quarterly art journal, *Art in Australia*. He opened the essay with a typically cheeky sentence: 'The writer is a layman who does not admit, as good Australian laymen apparently should, that he does not know much about art but he knows what he likes'.[8] He went on to explain that his 'complaint' was that any Australian with an interest in fine art or sculpture was unable to view the best contemporary examples in any of the public galleries. This, he claimed, was because of a perception that 'European painting ceased to be interesting in the nineties with the work of the French Impressionists and that there are no living sculptors of note. The distressing aspect of the matter is that there seems to be little chance of representative contemporary work appearing in [Australian] galleries for another quarter of a century. The layman is tacitly informed that if he wants to see such work he can go to London, New York, Essen or Moscow.' He urged the trustees responsible for purchasing works of art to shed their prejudices and buy more representative examples of contemporary art. The thrust of Long's article was at home in the avant-garde journal, which was generally supportive of contemporary art.

During 1933, Long was spending a good deal of time in the company of landscape artist and political cartoonist Miles Evergood, who he counted as a close friend. He especially admired Evergood's Australian landscape painting. The following paragraph from a 1500-word essay he wrote for *Art in Australia* magazine in April 1933 illustrates how seriously and confidently he approached the specialist field of art appreciation and how, as with film, he was keen to see Australia and Australians represented in the arts:

> Post-impressionism has hardly a representative among landscape painters in Australia. That is why the sudden appearance of a painting by Mr. Evergood – 'Howard Smith's Wharf, Brisbane' – among the entries for the Wynne Prize last February was, to my mind, so revealing and so provoking. It belongs to a kind of painting that Australian landscape has hardly known, for Australian landscape painting skipped with one bound from the cautious, dilūted impressionism of the generation which Arthur Streeton led to the tentative essays in cubist-classicism that a number of the younger painters are now producing.[9]

In 1939, Long wrote a letter to his mother from London, which gives a glimpse into his active, well-educated mind:

> This is a strange visit to England for me … because last time I was young, with full sympathy for the writers, painters, etc, then in their thirties and forties who were the revolutionaries of 15 years ago. But since then a new generation has grown up. Auden, Isherwood, MacNeice, Day Lewis, etc, are all or mostly younger than me. Living the restricted intellectual life that Australia imposes (or does this fault not lie in our stars) one found oneself consolidating one's position among the poets and painters of yesterday and the day before, going unsympathetic with the new generation. But that would be a foolish policy to pursue here, with the opportunity offered of seeing experimental plays, truly contemporary painting. So I am setting out to explore the mind of the younger generation.[10]

Throughout his life, Long maintained his interest in the arts and returned to art criticism and commentary with an essay for *Meanjin Quarterly* in 1964 entitled 'Young Paterson and young Lawson', focusing on the published poetry of Paterson in *the Bulletin* during the late 1880s and early 1890s.

Gavin's mother-in-law, a Barton, had for many years referred to Paterson as 'cousin Barty' (Banjo's given names were Andrew Barton). Lamenting that the volumes of collected verse available at that time failed to do justice to either of them, she believed 'readers deserve to know, and the critics need to know, far more about what they wrote and when'. Refusing to be drawn on the question of who was the better poet, Long offered that 'their verse would probably nowadays be considered about equal in quality'. Against the theory that Lawson was more concerned with poverty and social justice than Paterson, Long believed 'Paterson was more sharply aware of the problems of society and of contemporary politics than was Lawson. Paterson's radicalism was more intellectual than Lawson's, Lawson's more emotional than Paterson's.'[11] As to the influence of Kipling, citing several examples, he puts paid to the notion by pointing out that both were well into their stride before they had the chance to even read Kipling, and that some of Kipling's verse, supposedly influential on Paterson, was actually published after Paterson's.

The year 1930 had begun well for the Longs, but things unexpectedly took a turn for the worse. Gavin and Jocie now had a daughter, Jenifer, born on 4 February the previous year. Gavin was now on a senior reporter's salary and he finally got his driver's licence, although he very rarely used it. Then, in March, they enjoyed a visit from Gavin's parents, whose P&O ship, bound for London, docked briefly in Melbourne. The bishop, as energetic and active as ever, was on his way to the Lambeth Conference to oversee important reforms he was sponsoring for the Church of England in Australia. Gavin could not know at the time that this would be the last time he would see his father. On 9 July, a few days after suffering a massive stroke, George Long died. The following day, Gavin's beloved Maths Master from his Bathurst days, WR Brown, telegrammed his sympathies on the passing of his dear father.

For a year that had dawned with such promise, it was suddenly a bad time for Gavin Long. While holidaying in Sydney, the Longs received news of the bishop's death. And with the Depression taking its toll, the *Argus*, like many others, began taking drastic measures, sacking some staff and demoting others. Long was not dismissed, but he was demoted. He was now responsible for court reporting, which he found tedious and unsatisfying. He was also now fulfilling the responsibilities of co-executor of his father's estate, with all 3353 pounds bequeathed to his mother. In October, Gavin Long splurged nine pounds and 13 shillings to fly on the Southern Cloud to Sydney, embarked on the train to Newcastle and assisted his mother in adjusting to her new life as a widow. While in Sydney, he put out some feelers about a possible position at the *Sydney Morning Herald*. After returning to Melbourne, he spent the remainder of 1930 continuing to write for the *Argus*, but his ambitions now lay elsewhere.

In January 1931, he was further demoted to a general reporter. It was less disastrous than being sacked, but a blow nonetheless. In May, with Jenifer in the care of family friends, Gavin and Jocie took a brief walking tour near Dixon's Creek to regroup and discuss their options for the future. Gavin felt the need to move closer to Newcastle to be near his mother, and the employment situation in Melbourne showed no signs of improving. But almost immediately after their return home, everything changed. A telegram arrived from the *Sydney Morning Herald* offering him a job as a senior reporter.

On 4 July, the little family embarked on the SS *Karoola* for Sydney. With the prospects of a good job awaiting him in Sydney and the opportunity to be closer to his mother, even a very rough passage could not dampen Gavin Long's buoyed spirits. In fact, family lore has it that their son, Jeremy, born the following April, was conceived on that voyage.

Following a memorial service at St Mark's Darling Point on the first anniversary of his father's death, Long began work as a senior reporter at the *Herald* and joined the Federal Council of the Australian Journalists' Association. The *Herald* was a good fit for him, both temperamentally and professionally. According to Gavin Souter, the news columns of the

*Herald* during the first half of the 1930s were 'thorough and reliable, but there was little sparkle to them'. But the *Herald* was changing. There were new challenges, new technologies and a new energy that Long's strengths were well suited to. The *Herald's* chief competition, the *Daily Telegraph*, carved out its niche with a more flamboyant, often sensational style, some of which may have appealed to Long's creativity, but would soon have grated upon his more serious, sober sensibilities. His deft touch and more modern outlook qualified him as one of the new breed of journalists at the *Herald* in the 1930s who were beginning to replace the old guard. He ably combined serious journalistic professionalism with a forward-looking, fresh approach.

Gavin Long wrote occasional articles about foreign affairs and defence. 'These subjects had been my chief private interest', he later told John Hetherington. 'In 1936, I was appointed chief cable sub-editor, and the amount of my writings on defence increased: the idea that war was coming had begun to penetrate.' Again, with his appointment to chief cable sub-editor, Long was in the right place at the right time to make a solid contribution. And he was in an ideal position to view the foment of war from both an Australian and an international perspective as he was now handling daily cable news from overseas. He began working on a manuscript for a book about an invasion of Australia by Japan in 1940, a project he returned to through the years but was never to complete.

He applied a keen sense of history to his commentaries on Australian life, musing through the years about the uniquely Australian 'character'. National self-examination, widespread in Australian society after Federation and the Great War, was of enduring interest to him. Having been born into the new Federation and coming of age as his nation was being tested in war, Long was in that cohort of thinkers and writers who were personally invested in the enquiry.

He frequently reflected on national character and identity and tended to view these through the lens of Australian soldiery. His thought process ran almost in a straight line from the character of Australians in general to the character of Australian soldiers in particular, and then back the other way. What kinds of soldiers did Australia produce? And, conversely, what influence did Australian soldiery have on Australian society, its mores and perceptions of itself? In these enquiries, he was heavily influenced by Bean and, for Bean, the war of 1914–18 was 'a study and celebration of what he saw as the Australian character'.[12]

Long had his own ideas about the peculiar 'Australian-ness' of the Australian soldier, but the topic was not new. In 1896, Major General Edward 'Curly' Hutton, who a few years later would be appointed the first commander of the newly formed Australian Army, addressed the British Military Society at Aldershot. Hutton, a career officer, an imperialist at heart and a colourful speech-maker, drew upon first-hand experience to laud the characteristics and prowess of Australian soldiers:

> Fine horsemen, hardy, self-reliant, and excellent marksmen, they are the beau ideal of Mounted Riflemen … Accustomed to shift for themselves in the Australian bush, and under the most trying conditions of heat and cold, they would thrive where soldiers unaccustomed to bush life would die. If Australian soldiers, with their quick intelligence and strong individuality, fall into the hands of weak, ignorant and incapable officers, not only will indiscipline supervene, but the very individuality I speak of will prompt the men themselves to take matters into their own hands. No man, be he Cromwell or Napoleon, could *drive* Australian troops, but a strong and capable leader, no matter how strict could *lead* an Australian army to emulate – aye, and surpass if need be – the finest and most heroic deeds recorded in the annals of British arms.[13]

Bean elaborated on these themes in his official history and subsequent forums. In 1927, in an article for the *Journal of the Australian Historical Society*, Bean summarised his conclusions about Australian soldiers and their effect on Australian society and wrote that it is always dangerous to generalise, then proceeded to do exactly that. Adopting the role of psychologist, he stated that:

> [On the battlefield] one saw men with their innermost nature exposed … we had 300 000 Australians working beside several

> millions of others providing comparisons internationally and even a few broad distinctions between [men from Australian states]. Inasmuch as they [the AIF] were just a fair cross-section of our people, a study of their qualities may give us sidelights upon our national character.[14]

He described four qualities. First, a capacity for discipline. Not an unthinking and uneducated obeisance to rank, but the certainty that any order tending to the winning of the war would be obeyed. Although in the early days, Australian soldiers often felt entitled to ask 'why' before carrying it out. Second, an eagerness to learn:

> Again and again it was noted that, if there were ten Australians in a school of one hundred men taken from all sources in the British and Dominion forces, the majority of Australians would pass out near the top of the class, several of them often at the very top.

Third, Australian soldiers demonstrated a willingness to take a chance, to 'give it a go', to live heartily whenever they could, to make friends and look out for their mates. And finally, there emerged regimental differences between those who were 'bush-bred' or 'town-bred', attributing superiority to the former. Bean concluded with a plea for the preservation of conditions in Australian cities that approximate those of the countryside – outdoor living, exercise, parks, playgrounds, etc.

Long clearly absorbed a great deal of this. Correspondence between Bean and Long in June 1930 gives an indication of their thinking on the subject. At the time, Long was a newly promoted sub-editor for the *Argus*, a role he described as a 'pleasantly uneventful occupation and a change from the mixed pleasures of reporting', but one which did not inspire or challenge him; rather, it provided him ample time to think. He wrote to Bean – for many years his letters were addressed 'Dear Dr. Bean'; it was not until the 1950s that he began to address him as 'Charles' – lavishly praising his recently published volumes of history and lamenting the fact that the soldiers who reminisced publicly about the 1914–18 war had become 'a popular object of ridicule to the post-war generation'. He continued revealingly: 'I am convinced that an honest and civilised man must be a pacifist and anti-patriotic today. But if the AIF is not enshrined as it deserves to be in our history nothing will be left of it soon but a caricature and a phantom.' Long was clearly not interested in jingoism – that which masquerades as 'patriotism' and can so often descend into warmongering. He honoured soldiering while advocating pacifism. He was concerned that a dearth of knowledge about the Australian sons and daughters who went to that war, and the resultant myths and legends that grew up about them, could only dishonour them and impede the positive development of Australian society.

Bean's quest for 'the true man not the superman' obviously resonated with Long. In 1942, about a year after returning from the Middle East, Long wrote a piece for the *Sydney Morning Herald* entitled 'The comic-paper digger':

> A generation of Australians for some inscrutable reason, were taught that the typical Australian soldier was a concave, tipsy lounger with a cigarette drooping from his hawk-like face, who called the colonel by his Christian name, charged furiously with the bayonet in battle, and spent the rest of his time breaking and boozing.[15]

He noted that the image had been clinging to the Australian Army for more than 20 years, having taken root and flourished in the minds of the generation that lived between the wars – a generation with little first-hand knowledge of the reality. By 1939, aspects of this legend had even infected officers who thought that 'Australian soldiers had to be cajoled not commanded'. It only took a campaign or two for it to become obvious that 'those who approximate the comic-paper Digger invariably made bad soldiers' and that 'a battle demanded an entirely different kind of courage to that which was needed in a bar-room brawl'.

In 1943, further developing these thoughts, and in response to a piece in *Yank, the Army Weekly* published in New York, he wrote an essay entitled 'The real Australian soldier' for the *Infantry Journal*, which was then re-published as an illustrated pamphlet by the Australian News and Information Bureau.

'There is a picturesque legend that dies hard', he wrote. The soldier is a 'wild, undisciplined fighting man, a six-footer, standing in torn and dirty uniform, rifle in one hand and bottle of beer in the other, cussing a blue streak and beating hell out of anything that comes along'. He was at pains to put paid to this caricature. And one can only imagine that there were many Australians in uniform who were grateful.

Gavin Long believed that Australian service personnel had earned the right to be judged for the reality rather than revered or maligned for the legend. For Long, and Bean before him, the legend too easily masks, warps or belittles reality. He wanted us to acknowledge and appreciate the Australian soldier, knowing that new replacements from Australia who fancied themselves in the mould of the mythical 'rifle in one hand and bottle of beer in the other' were not at all desirable to the fighting units they were destined to join.

Long's commentary on Australian soldiery matured. In his presentation to the 1952 Australian and New Zealand Association for the Advancement of Science, called 'Problems of Australian military cooperation with other military forces', he highlighted the difficulties that arose for a small national partner such as Australia when operating in a multinational military alliance. [16] His thesis was that military forces display national characteristics, which should be taken into account by those engaged in such operations to improve efficiencies and minimise avoidable misunderstandings.

Long proposed that 'armies derive their character from the nations that produce them; the soldier may not be molded by the drill sergeant into somebody entirely different from what he was.'[17] To this, he added a caveat. Ever an Army man, and aware of his limited experience with other branches of the service, he acknowledged that he had 'tried to uncover some useful avenues of enquiry and to do so strictly in the army', adding that matters of national character may play out differently in the significantly different structures and organisation of air forces and navies.

He further argued that the soldier may be shaped 'by the home and by the school as much as by the barracks and the bivouac'. To that end, he referred to the effects of social expectations on the strengths or weaknesses of an army. He noted that an

> army of peasants will be less troubled by hardships which would appal an army drawn from a highly mechanised community – in one nation's army, the absence of a field laundry may be felt as a greater privation than, in another, the necessity to march on bare feet. An army of European colonials will be capable of improvisation and economy of means bewildering to soldiers derived from more static and stratified societies.

He then pointed to the influence of national or social structure on the way nations traditionally go about choosing regimental officers – the British relying heavily upon class, the Americans on their aristocracy and the Australians on a volunteer cadre representing 'a large number of social and economic groups'. These structural differences and the assumptions underlying them directly affect expectations regarding discipline. Long cited British assumptions in the Great War that Australians may make good fighters but not good soldiers because they seemed to care less about British traditional notions of discipline. 'Australian officers were realists and, provided troops were clean and their guns and transport fit for any action, they did not usually insist that buttons must shine, hubs and chains sparkle, and martingales be pipe-clayed.'

Again citing Bean, he observed that colonial forces in 1918 – Australian, New Zealand and Canadian – 'had been the best in the field, an opinion later supported by authoritative German and British investigators, including the British official historian'. Yet, in material respects, the Australian forces had often failed to observe European traditions: notions of discipline, the death penalty and the boundary separating the classes from which officers and ranks were drawn.

Long offered a further example of what he saw as a national characteristic relating to idiosyncrasies of language and communication.

He cited General Mackay's lament in 1941 that Australian officers had been sloppy and ambiguous and prone to exaggeration in communications and reports. By contrast, when he liaised with General MacArthur's headquarters in Brisbane, Long was surprised to hear officers being berated for not exaggerating enough! 'The British habit is to err on the side of under-statement, the American habit is to express himself with emphasis perhaps even flamboyantly.' Then there was the time American staff officers were confused by an Australian report that an exhausted coast watcher was 'knocked up'.

He concluded his address by listing some Australian characteristics to be taken into account by those who are engaged in multinational forces – arising from the fact that Australia is a distinctly egalitarian society – such as resentment sparked by 'officers only' beaches. And because of the value placed on independence of thought, Australians tend to be inquisitive. As a result, Australian soldiers are more likely to give their best if they are kept well informed. They want to know what is going on. This inquisitiveness can lead to a perception of unruliness.

Long was less forthcoming in public when commenting on the reverse process – the way Australian soldiery influenced the character of the wider Australian citizenry. He did, however, express himself privately. In a letter to Bean in 1944, he spoke admiringly of what he called 'the digger's law' of toleration and comradeship as key to the postwar changes that Australia would have to navigate:

> Although religion has lost some of its force, I do not think that the younger generation is without a guiding light or that we need have any fears about its qualities. Thou shalt love thy neighbour as thyself, is, I think, the diggers law. The digger's performance and his wife's could not have come from a background gravely lacking in ethical standards. Why did the Australians go to the war in 1939–40? Some say they were restless and adventurous and that's a reason the men themselves often give, but they were men of a certain type – the blokes who stand up in trains. I think war has strengthened their virtues. We are going to have more and larger industrial resettlements before it is over. If the soldier

> is to be brought safely home again it will need much toleration and comradeship (even between the people of Rose Bay and those in Balmain) and much of his own brand of Christianity in high places to do it. It's only in leadership we can fail, and I don't think we will finally. We haven't so far.[18]

But Long's social commentary about Australian soldiery was not his prime remit. By 1938, he had become, according to historian Robert Moss, 'in effect, the first peacetime defence correspondent in Australia', which necessarily entailed engaging in overtly political commentary. Midway through that year, the *Herald's* new editor, McClure Smith, was staking out the newspaper's popular, though somewhat controversial, position against European appeasement of Hitler. The United Australia Party (UAP) was arguing for reliance on Britain, and the Labor Party was reluctant to engage with growing martial tensions in Europe and Asia, but Long published the view that Australia had lagged dangerously behind in its capacity for self-defence and needed to spend more on equipment and training.

He had been paying attention to those voices from within the Australian armed forces that had, since the 1920s, been warning about the vulnerability of 'Fortress Singapore' to a land-based attack by the Japanese. He was very keen, therefore, to accept the opportunity to travel with the Governor-General, Lord Gowrie, on a goodwill visit to Java and Singapore during March and April of 1938 and to write about the defence readiness of the Dutch East Indies and Singapore. 'This was in the days when people were wondering what Japan was going to do and it was on the march. I think I was pretty sure war was coming,' he later told Bruce Juddery, who wrote in the *Canberra Times* that although Long was not the first Australian to sound warnings about the vulnerability of Singapore, 'he was the first journalist to do so in a daily newspaper'.[19]

In February 1938, he found himself reporting from HMAS *Australia* during an Australia–New Zealand exercise. He outlined six requirements that he felt Australia would need to secure to defend herself in the region against 'minor raids', including bombardment from the sea: a strong Empire fleet based nearby; an adequate Australian navy of ships to cruiser size, essentially for coastal and anti-submarine defence; strategically placed coastal heavy guns; sufficient troops to protect important centres from enemy raiding parties; anti-aircraft guns; and shore-based aircraft. 'Essentially bound up with these requirements,' he wrote, 'are the manufacture of munitions and other war materials, the coordination of industry and supply, and such other forms of effort as may conduce to an efficient scheme of local defence'.[20] He wrote the following day that there was an 'obvious risk' involved, given Australia's vast coastline and 'the uncertainty of the international situation' in not planning to immediately increase Australia's small fleet of three ageing cruisers.

Throughout 1938, Long would write some 60 000 words on defence matters, covering the political, military and social aspects of a country that was ill-prepared for the war that was soon to come. He published articles that went far beyond merely reporting the state of play; rather, they offered specific, well-considered solutions and plans for training, recruitment, equipment supplies and facilities that would have helped prepare the nation for war had they been heeded.

One example of Long's capacity for marshalling facts and using them to mount a cogent, unflinching argument is found in an article he wrote in November 1938 under the headline 'Gaps in our defences – Weapons and men lacking – Facts which must be faced'. In this bold opinion piece, he countered UAP Leader and PM Joseph Lyons' criticisms: 'Mr. Lyons complained of critics who were "unarmed with facts" and replied making a statement of his own in which relevant facts were conspicuously lacking and comfortable generalisations abounded'.[21]

Long went on to provide a detailed rebuttal of Lyons' 'placid generalisations'. Regarding land forces, he wrote: 'When rearmament began four years ago, army leaders impressed upon the Cabinet that the need for equipment was so urgent that it should be given priority. Mr. Lyons promised to raise the strength of the militia to 70,000.' Long argued that there was

> the need for vastly more regular officers and instructors to make the training of the hoped-for militiamen effective. Without a regular force, ready for immediate service, and made mobile by mechanical vehicles, Australia has no land force with which to meet an attack. 'Equipment exists for the mobilisation of seven divisions,' says Mr. Lyons, but he omits to say that most of it was inherited from the AIF and that many other necessities of modern warfare are still missing entirely … after four years of rearmament. Mr. Lyons states that 'a new development is the manufacture of anti-aircraft guns at Maribyrnong.' Yet they have been in development since 1935 and only six anti-aircraft guns are in the Newcastle-Sydney-Port Kembla area and four of those are imported guns acquired years ago. Neither the Hawker Demons nor the Avro Ansons are genuinely modern fighting aircraft and any air force which uses them in fighter or bomber squadrons knows that it is using makeshifts. Mr. Lyons did not explain what factors have decided that no better machines than these should be in Australia.

By August 1938, the demands of travel, sub-editing and writing had begun to take their toll on Gavin Long. After returning from a brief family holiday, he succumbed to a month-long illness. In early November, he wrote to Bean:

> The last three years have been extremely strenuous. For more than a year, I've combined senior cable editor with writer on military and naval subjects as 'special representative' or 'our defence correspondent' or as a leader writer. This has meant writing about 60,000 words of discussion of these somewhat dangerous subjects and a good deal of straight reporting as well.

But Long's industry and talent as defence correspondent had not gone unnoticed at the *Herald*, and towards the end of that year, he was offered a posting to the paper's Overseas News Service London office. This would prove a decisive turn in his career as it placed him in London in 1939 and in a prime position to report the outbreak of war in September of that year. He was also perfectly placed to become the *Herald*'s war correspondent with the ill-fated British Expeditionary Force in Western Europe and to endure his first evacuation under fire.

# 4
# OUR OWN CORRESPONDENT

*The town from which I am writing has been machine-gunned and bombed at intervals tonight and half-a-dozen buildings are blazing. There are intervals of silence then a rapid pounding of anti-aircraft guns and pom-poms, followed by the crashing of a line of bombs.*

– Gavin Long[1]

On 9 January 1939, Gavin and Jocelyn Long, with their children, Jenifer and Jeremy, aged nine and six years, disembarked from the SS *Moreton Bay* in pouring rain at Southampton. They had sailed from Sydney via Colombo. They travelled by train to their new 'digs' in a boarding house on Albermarle Road, Beckenham in South London. This would be their home until bombers of the Third Reich appeared in the skies in 1940. Long was set to take up duties, initially for two years, at the cable office of the *Sydney Morning Herald* in Fleet Street.

Before leaving Australia, Gavin described the appointment in a letter to Charles Bean, explaining that the Australian Associated Press service was being reduced in scope and the supplementary service that it shared with *The Age* was being increased. At that time, the London office consisted of two men, cable editor Tahu Hole and manager Gordon Gilmour. Long was appointed to assist because of his experience handling cables. He was eager for the new challenge. His work at the *Herald* had become onerous. While serving as senior cable sub-editor, he was also regularly producing 'straight reporting' and writing on complex and sometimes politically sensitive defence matters – he referred to them as 'dangerous subjects' – under the guise of 'special representative' or 'defence correspondent'. He was ready for a change and understandably thrilled to be chosen for the important

London post. To Bean, he had lamented, 'I am beginning to feel that I have taught my off-siders [*sic*] here all I know and am beginning to feel like an old fogey'.[2]

While traversing the Red Sea en route to Southampton, he wrote a somewhat poetic letter to his mother, who may have felt that his missives sometimes resembled pieces he supplied to weekend magazines:

> An oily sea, but a cooler day than we expected after a sweltering night. Colombo: The kids thoroughly enjoyed their first glimpse of the East – the bullock carts, bright costumes, coconut palms, catamarans, rickshaws. Then we set off across the Arabian Sea towards Aden.[3]

He then captured something of the adventure this sea journey was for the family, especially the children:

> It is a good experience in that it is making them more independent and sociable. Nowhere except on a ship could children be thrown so close together with people of so many ages. In three days at the most we will be out of the tropical heat of the Red Sea and into a European winter of uncommon severity.

Indeed, the Long family arrived to the coldest, wettest year in the south of England for a decade.

These were lean times for the family. Gavin's first pay cheque was not due until 1 February. They faced added financial concerns when he was informed that difficulties in establishing the cable link to Sydney meant his commencement would be delayed indefinitely. As it turned out, the cable service commenced on 12 February, but with a reduced staff of three, not the expected four. This resulted in the need to work alternate weekly shifts commencing at 6 am and 4 am.

It transpired that one and sometimes both of his colleagues were less than reliable, resulting in an effective staff of just two, sometimes only one. He began the work single-handedly on that first day as one of his colleagues was away sick and the other hungover from getting 'frightfully shot' the night before. The work was hard and lonely, with terrible hours, sometimes 'awfully hectic', and included night shifts. In a letter to his mother, he explained that his work and that of his fellow correspondents was to 'send out to the Herald the messages that are marked "From Our Own Correspondent". Generally speaking, the Australian Associated Press, the A.A.P., have a look at the morning's cables – sends out the bare bones of the news, and we try to explain to you what it is all about'.

To avoid the disruption of rising so early to get to the office, he took lodgings in a small, dreary attic room in Taviton Street, convenient to Euston Station. This arrangement cost 24 shillings and 6 pence a week. Meanwhile, Jocie established as much of a routine as she could: overseeing the schooling of Jenifer and Jeremy each morning; visiting the local picture theatre each Monday afternoon, jotting down her critique of each film in her diary; and attending to domestic duties. She regularly travelled by train into town from Beckenham Station, visiting shops and meeting friends for coffee.[4]

During this time, Long met and struck up a friendship with recently retired naval officer, Captain Russell Grenfell, RN. Long admired Grenfell as an author and historian and the pair quickly discovered they shared similar views on Singapore's vulnerability to Japanese attack. They began to collaborate on a book that Long had been quietly drafting since 1936, envisaging such an attack from the Malay Peninsula while the British fleet was elsewhere. In Long's original conception, the Japanese invasion would come in 1940. The book was tentatively titled 'Defence Against Japan'. Long and Grenfell devoted considerable spare time to the project until they were interrupted by the war declaration in September after which Grenfell immediately returned to Royal Navy duty in Scotland and Long yearned to join the correspondents who would travel with the British Expeditionary Force (BEF) to the Continent. Jocelyn wrote to her mother that the 'bottom had been knocked out of [Gavin's] beloved book'. It was never published, although Long returned to it from time to time in subsequent years, transforming it into a short history entitled *Japan's Eight Years War*. Not long before his death in 1968, he finally abandoned the manuscript. It is currently held in the AWM archives.[5]

On 15 March 1939, amid rumours of impending war, Jocelyn wrote in her diary: 'Germany walked – or rather marched – into Prague today. The dirty cow. It was awful listening to the wireless news this evening and hearing how our Chamberlain has disclaimed all moral responsibility – as usual. It will be our turn soon I suppose.' Two days later, the Germans took Czechoslovakia and three weeks after that the Italians overran Dalmatia. Towards the end of March, Gavin bought an unexpurgated English version of Hitler's *Mein Kampf*, which both he and his wife read. Their impressions are not recorded.

Escalating Nazi belligerence led to an increasingly anxious time for many in England. On 7 April, Jocelyn noted fretfully in her diary: 'Some woman in Beckenham has stored loads of Macintosh's toffee in her cellar in case of war. Should I be a loyal wife and stay in England, or devoted mother and depart to USA or home while the going's good?'[6] Meanwhile, word had reached them from friends back home that 'anti-Japanese sentiment was sweeping Australia' and that men everywhere were expecting to be joining up for one war or another very soon. Gavin and Jocelyn began planning a visit to the Continent while the going was still good. On 9 April, Jocie wrote: 'I'm still hoping to get to Germany next week – if only things will hold off a bit. I'd love to be somewhere in Germany for Hitler's 50th birthday – Apr 20 – just to see how they celebrate it.' Gavin managed to secure some leave and, with the children safely in the care of their landlady, Mrs Bremberg, the couple spent three days visiting Holland and Germany. Jocelyn described the experience as 'Awfully Interesting'. She provided vivid details of their time in Cologne in a letter to her mother:

> I'd been feeling rather nervous about it, wondering if I'd have to do the Nazi salute or be thrown into concentration camps, and expected mild hostility from all sides. But nothing of the kind. Everything was Perfectly Ordinary! Really friendly. There were hardly any soldiers about, and what there were gave each other the ordinary military salute. No goosestepping! Even the Nazis

> just flapped their arms in greeting, often not even saying 'Heil', let alone 'Heil Hitler'.

Her recollections of the visit included a conversation with a German businessman who took them to dinner and the music hall:

> The German thinks that if only England would give Germany back her colonies – some of them – the tension would ease; in fact everything would be alright. He told us among other things that 'we're only slaves here you know. 65% of my earnings go in taxes'. I didn't like him very much but I finished up feeling extremely sorry for him, and for all the nice everyday people we encountered.

The pair had a foretaste of things to come on the return crossing. Jocelyn wrote to her mother about the wretched state of fleeing Jewish refugees on board the ferry: 'Coming home we encountered a mob of unfortunate German Jewish refugees on the boat. It was AWFUL. I was eventually reduced to horrid sickness just by the sights around us!'

At 9:30 am on 1 September, Long telephoned his wife from the third-floor *Herald* office in Fleet Street to tell her the Germans had just invaded Poland. Londoners heard the news half an hour later over the wireless. She wrote that her 'heart suddenly began thumping as Gavin talked – a horrid feeling'. Three days later, she and their children, ten-year-old Jenifer and seven-year-old Jeremy, joined the evacuation, leaving their boarding house in Beckenham for Cornwall. She observed:

> In the crowded train from Paddington, I sat opposite a notice: 'In the event of the train being splashed with mustard gas, oily smears may be visible on windows and door handles. Do not touch these surfaces or attempt to alight, but call the assistance of the platform staff who will have the door handles and floor boards decontaminated'.

Two days later, Australians heard the 'melancholy' news broadcast by Prime Minister Robert Menzies that 'in consequence of the persistence by Germany in her invasion of Poland, Great Britain has declared war upon her and that as a result Australia is also at war'. Australians were immediately hungry for news. Long took to sleeping in hotels and wherever he could find digs closer to the cable office to be on hand for the anticipated increase in cable activity. With the sudden establishment of censorship, the work of a journalist became more demanding, 'things having to be written more carefully and taking longer to get off'. He applied immediately to go to France as a designated war correspondent with the BEF, but continued to attend to cable traffic while he awaited assignment. Long's droll sense of humour and lively wit are evident in pieces he wrote in an unpublished account in the days before he embarked for France. On 13 September, for example:

> Nothing may be printed except with the approval of a Propaganda Ministry which differs from Germany's only in its fantastic inefficiency. Anything from 50 to 200 journalists are there receiving communiqués that simply don't mean a thing and which, in any case, have been broadcast long before they are handed out there. At one stage, a foreign newspaperman … waved his arms about and shouted 'Why don't they just install a radio!'[7]

And then:

> It's a grim kind of war. Our own planes have sunk at least one of our own submarines, our own guns have shot down at least two of our own planes, the Germans have mined at least one of their own torpedo boats. The Dutch have mined one of their own minesweepers … and three German freighters are ashore in the Baltic, presumably because they gave an excessively wide berth to their own minefields and forgot the other hazard. I've half a mind to call the whole thing off.

On 10 October, wearing khaki and an armband of broad black and white stripes emblazoned with the word 'PRESS' and with a portable typewriter in his kitbag, he shipped out from Southampton for France and Belgium. That same day, the *Sydney Morning Herald* announced Gavin Long's assignment, noting that he had long made a close study of defence and Allied subjects and, as the *Herald*'s defence correspondent in Australia, 'had previously written articles which attracted widespread attention'.

With a keen sense of both personal and global history, he wrote a letter to his mother:

> I have been reminded of 1917, when dad arrived home with kitbags full of khaki. I am only a few years younger than he was in 1917 and the men who will have to do the hardest work this time are the sons of the men who were also in their twenties last time.

In an attempt to allay her fears for his safety, he went on to describe the work he expected he would do 'quartered in a hotel or house very far from the German frontier, whence there will be excursions to see the sort of thing the army will imagine the newspapermen want to write about'.

The importance of the press in this new war quickly became evident. The commander of the BEF, Lord Gort, reported in despatches that the Press had, from the first day, begun to play a far more significant role than had been appreciated prior to the outbreak of hostilities. Gort noted the presence of about 50 war correspondents under his purview, as well as representatives of principal newsreel companies. In addition, upwards of 60 visiting editors, correspondents and cinematographers had been permitted to visit his force.

On 28 December 1939, Gavin Long was the first Australian war correspondent ever to receive a byline in the *Sydney Morning Herald*. His despatches from the frontline were also sometimes attributed in Australian newspapers to 'G.M. Long, our own correspondent in France', 'Our own correspondent with the B.E.F.' or 'Our special correspondent'. Gavin Souter, in his definitive history of the *Herald* –

*Company of Heralds* – erroneously attributed the first *Sydney Morning Herald* byline to war correspondent GEW Harriott in 1942.[8] In response to a letter from Long's son, Jeremy, in 1981, Souter conceded that, indeed, Gavin Long was the first to receive a byline.

There were Australians serving with the BEF and Long did his best to speak with them to include them in his stories. The equivalent of 16 fighter squadrons of the Royal Air Force (RAF) served with the BEF, and most of them contained an Australian or two. By the final months of 1939, there were already about 450 Australians serving in the RAF, almost all of them pilots.

It was not only pilots that he interviewed. On 26 October, Long reported on conversations he had with eight nurses in the British casualty clearing station not far from the line. They were keen and ready to serve. Three of these nurses were Australian, two from Victoria and one from NSW:

> They were working in England when war broke out and enlisted immediately. In this war, unlike the last, these sisters in casualty clearing stations will be equipped with steel helmets, in addition to gas masks and they will be well within the danger zone. The matron of this station had seen four years' service in France in the 1914–18 war, and stated that she was 'looking forward' to perhaps a few more years on the same battlefields.[9]

Long tirelessly traversed the Belgian and French landscape between October 1939 and January 1940 during the cold winter of the so-called 'phoney war'. He toured military installations, interviewed soldiers, airmen and civilians, and gleaned what stories he could for the readers in Australia. The lively prose of his frequent despatches belied the anticlimactic fact that very little of consequence was happening. He had no alternative but to write lengthy commentaries and observations about the weather, the countryside, and the activities and morale of the troops as they settled into defensive positions and dull routines. On 14 October he described the steady activity of a vast Allied army moving steadily to establish itself on the anticipated field of battle:

> Unobtrusively moving chiefly by night, camouflaged so that by day long lines of guns, cars and fighting vehicles merge with the brown and green and autumn tints of a French October landscape, a British army of 160,000 men, with its vehicles has occupied a wide tract of France and is fortifying its line.
>
> [we passed through] … towns whose names were made historic by the battles of the last war and past an occasional field of war graves whose ordered rows of headstones grimly recalled the battles fought on this soil by many who are serving again today with their sons fighting beside them.[10]

On 23 October he described the civilian population that watched:

> … civilian life is going on more normally than in London or Paris. There are towns in Devon and Cornwall where hardly a chink of light can be seen at night, but in towns here householders are less meticulous. Children in frontier villages are going to school as usual. Few buildings are sandbagged and only a small proportion of the populace has bothered to paste strips of brown paper across the windows. This suggests that people whose villages were devastated in the last war have become fatalistic and calm compared with populations whose experience is less grim.[11]

By November, and with the approach of winter, it seemed that an imminent German offensive was unlikely; nevertheless, the daily drudgery of preparing for it went on and there was precious little for the war correspondents to report:

> I stood last night in the mud watching the dim shapes of a working party putting up barbed wire entanglements. Doubtless our voices were for a while raised louder than necessary. Then a pistol shot split the silence, and a Verey light, soaring in the black sky from 'No Man's Land' 400 yards away beyond the tank obstacles, flooded the paddock with light and fell sizzling five

> yards from the wiring party, who crouched motionless trying to look like a hayrick.[12]

In Long's report of 10 November, he returned to a passionately held theme – Australia's unpreparedness for war. Throughout the 1930s, he had addressed this concern many times and now he lamented that very few Australian officers were attached to the BEF, even though there were sufficient Australian officers on attachment to British regiments at the time to have made it feasible for many of them to take part in and learn from the expedition. Long felt it was a missed opportunity for Australian officers to have been recalled home at the outbreak of war and he beseeched the Australian Government to send some of them now to France:

> The price Australia has paid has been the loss of adequate, first-hand experience of the vast job now being done here. Never before has so large an army of mechanised and motorised troops been moved so far by sea and land. Valuable experience can be shared with the Dominions only at second-hand unless Dominion officers are sent to France.[13]

On 22 November, Long opined optimistically and, we now know, naively, that the preparation time afforded the Allied armies during the uneventful winter would easily vanquish a German advance the following spring. He predicted that 'by next March, the English and French armies will have been enormously strengthened and the Germans will face a combined army they could not hope to defeat'.[14] Few anticipated then that, by May, the Germans would identify the weakest section of the Allied defences and exploit it with devastating effect.

On 25 November, Gavin Long returned to London on leave. The next day, Jocie wrote in her diary: 'G. on a few days leave in Folkstone, Regent Palace Hotel, London. We met up on the platform in the twilight. Neither of us was quite sure we'd found the right person.' They dined at the expensive Hotel Grill 'on the Fairfax's' – steaks, sherry, burgundy, liqueur – 'but it was wasted on us really'. And over the next few days: 'had a very good dinner at the public restaurant for 3/6, including dancing; went with friends to the Hippodrome to see 'Black Velvet'. G got a raise from £13.10 to £16.'

On 30 November, Long flew back to Paris, dozed in a music hall throughout the afternoon and then travelled by train to his billet 'somewhere in France'. During his brief sojourn, it seems he had reconsidered his article of 21 November about the futility of a German armoured push in the spring. His article, published on 30 November, was prescient:

> Tanks with the help of low-flying fighter and bomber planes certainly won the war in Poland. One can picture an unexpected attack, not by dozens, but by hundreds of tanks at a sector of the line where the tanks will outnumber the anti-tank guns. The attack will be supported by forces of fast light tanks which will rumble swiftly through the gap cut by the cruiser tanks and make havoc.[15]

His December despatches betrayed the growing frustration of a diligent war correspondent as he endeavoured to compose daily reports from a vast theatre as yet devoid of battle. He was reduced to noting that an Alsatian dog had been killed during an Allied patrol and that a British soldier had fired a rifle grenade in the night when the jam tin attached to the barbed wire entanglement rattled. 'Britain's first shot was fired towards the noise and disturbed the enemy marauder – possibly a feeding rabbit.'

On 26 and 27 December, with nothing else to report, Long wrote an extensive piece about reporting! He provided a detailed explanation of the apparatus of wartime news gathering and the dilemmas faced by journalists under a censorious wartime regime. He then produced a 1500-word piece about the intricacies of the construction of the Maginot Line.

On 30 December, Jocelyn wrote in her diary that she had received a letter from Gavin to say he had been very ill, that he almost got pneumonia but was now okay, and was expecting to leave France about the end of January. She added wryly, 'The only comfort I've had all this time has been knowing that he probably wasn't dead or someone would have let me know'.

There being so little of consequence for Long to report, the *Herald* recalled him. On 8 January, he went by train to the Channel Coast and embarked on the ferry the next morning for the crossing, complete with a destroyer escort. He returned to snowy London to resume duties at the cable office. Glad to be reunited with his wife – the children continued at boarding school in Cornwall – he dutifully settled back to the daily grind of cable editing at Fleet Street. Jocelyn wrote:

> We're all living the old pre-war life at the moment. But if air raids begin I'll have to take the children away. And the moment things begin to happen in France, Gavin will presumably be sent over again. It's a queer background to life, for people like us who are used to being if anything, too fixed.

Then came an unexpected invitation, the substance and outcome of which sheds light upon the talent and character of Gavin Long.

On 21 January, he was summoned to Australia House to be interviewed by Australian High Commissioner and former Australian prime minister Stanley Bruce, who had received a cable from the Australian Government inviting Long to apply for the role of Australian Commonwealth Official War Correspondent with the Second AIF. Prime Minister Menzies, impressed by Long's reporting as defence correspondent throughout 1938, wanted him for the role and unofficially asked the *Herald* if Long could be made available. Bruce reassured Long that Rupert Henderson, General Manager at the *Herald*, had agreed to release him if he was appointed to the role and to take him back onto the staff once it was complete. Long told Bruce he was delighted to 'accept the offer if it were made'. The role seemed perfect for him. Indeed, it would have represented a logical and pleasing succession, and Long's mentor, none other than Charles Bean himself, privately endorsed the proposal.

The role of official correspondent was widely advertised in Australia. One of the requirements of the successful appointee would be that he would keep diaries throughout the war, preparatory to writing the official history when the war ended.[16] Fifty applicants were chosen and required to submit three articles to a panel comprising Sir Henry Gullett, Minister for Information; TW Brennan; KC Percy Jenkins, Chief Publicity Censor; and Charles Bean.

According to Clement Semmler, editor of Slessor's war diaries, Gullett was a keen supporter of one candidate – journalist and poet Kenneth Slessor, who was at the time the editor of the idiosyncratic *Smith's Weekly*. Following the panel's deliberations, Gullett announced to the Cabinet that Slessor had been selected unanimously. It is hardly credible that Bean would have endorsed Slessor over Long. Perhaps the recommendation was not unanimous, or perhaps Gavin's name had not been presented to the panel for consideration after all. Perhaps Gullett was being disingenuous.

Meanwhile, in London, Long and his wife had been waiting anxiously for news of the appointment. Jocie recorded in her diary that they both privately suspected that Sir Keith Murdoch would put pressure on the government to have 'his man' – meaning Slessor – appointed to the position. 'If only we didn't both want it so much!' she lamented. Meanwhile, back at the *Herald* office in Sydney, rumours had begun to circulate that Slessor would be appointed. Menzies, on hearing this from *Herald* news editor Angus McLachlan, is said to have remarked, 'I would as soon appoint Lennie Lower!'[17]

The rumours were eventually silenced. On 11 April, Long was alerted by a friend about a Dutch radio broadcast out of Australia that announced the appointment of a 'Kenneth Sheffield' – Slessor – to the important role. And here, we catch a glimpse of the man, Gavin Long. In a conversation with his wife, as she records it, he responded to this very hard news with his usual humility and generosity, commenting to her that Slessor was, in his opinion, 'one of the four best journalists in Australia' – a generous assessment indeed! One wonders which four journalists Long had in mind and, indeed, if he himself was one of them.

As fate would have it, another opportunity presented itself on the very same day. He had long been seeking approval from the Admiralty, and finally received it, to spend time at sea aboard some of His Majesty's ships to report on their activities. He was granted permission to board a minesweeper out of Harwich and report on the activities of the Royal Navy in the North Sea. He packed a toothbrush and typewriter and went off to meet the ship, expecting to be away overnight. The next day, his colleague at the cable office, Gordon Gilmour, received a note from Long saying not to expect him for several days and 'would you please tell my wife'. He made several trips with convoys from Scotland over subsequent weeks but was back in London on the fateful Friday of 10 May 1940.

# 5

# A FAIRLY STRENUOUS TIME

*Official records can be rather bald but can be enlivened by first-hand accounts.*

Gavin Long[1]

At dawn on 10 May 1940, German armoured forces smashed into France, Luxembourg, Holland and Belgium. They advanced quickly through the dense Ardennes forest to attack along that section of French territory not defended by the Maginot Line. British, French and Belgian armies reacted swiftly, moving into defensive positions and forming a front along the Dyle River from Sedan in the south to Antwerp in the north. Gavin Long hurriedly left London for Southampton, bound once again for France. It was to be a brief, frenetic and dangerous tour ending with evacuation under fire just 11 days later.

Between 4:30 am and 9 pm on Saturday 11 May, Gavin Long made the arduous journey from Arras to Lille in northern France and joined correspondents who had been at BEF General Headquarters the day before and had been startled awake early that morning by bombs dropping on the nearby aerodrome. From Lille, he wrote to Jocelyn:

> I left my bag behind and came on here with my toothbrush etc in a haversack and we have all been here ever since. The bombed houses, the charred wrecks of planes and the constant stream of troops and lorries and tanks seem grimmer than ever. I borrowed a pair of pyjamas from a colleague. I'd be glad if you posted over those shoes.[2]

He could not have foreseen that he would be forced to depart from France before he could receive those shoes.

Just seven days later, he and thousands of other non-combatants were caught up in an increasingly desperate retreat from the advancing Germans and then hastily evacuated to England. In typical fashion, he later described that period as 'a fairly strenuous time'. All that week, he and his colleagues were only a day or two ahead of the Germans, receiving order after order to fall further back. They stoically endured nights of broken sleep and days of too little food, and a growing sense of how deadly things had quickly become.

The Germans attacked with three army groups, comprising a total of 89 divisions, ten of them armoured, with co-ordinated air support and with 45 divisions in reserve. On 13 May, as von Rundstedt's tanks were pushing westward over the Meuse, surprising almost everyone with the devastating speed of their advance, Long set out from Lille by car at 3 pm in the company of another correspondent and a conducting officer on a long reconnoitre through Belgium. In perfect spring weather, passing bombed houses and the charred wrecks of planes, they were able to drive to Louvain and Wavre, doing their best to keep clear of a 'constant stream of troops and lorries and tanks' as well as countless Belgian refugees straggling back.

They continued throughout the night and returned at about 5 am 'after having had half an hour's sleep in the car at the side of the road'. He immediately set to work, typing his tightly scribbled notes into a report that had to be ready for transmission by 7 am. His accounts of his experiences that week, published almost daily in Australia, represent compelling eyewitness reporting that gives a sense of the terrible drama that rapidly unfolded.

Under the byline 'G.M. Long' or, sometimes, 'Our Special Correspondent', he provided *Herald* readers with vivid descriptions of what he witnessed. He wrote about Heinkel and junkers bombers destroying Belgian houses and 'shattering acres of window glass'.[3] He described processions of refugees heading south towards France in lorries and cars and 'on bicycles with a pathetic little bundle of clothing or food on the carrier, some with children on the handle bars' with 'here and there Boy Scouts directing traffic through towns and along main roads'.[4] He recounted a conversation with a 22-year-old Australian fighter pilot who claimed that the slow-flying German bombers were 'the easiest things to shoot down'[5], adding that it was 'dashed good fun provided you get a decent rest now and then'.

Between 14 and 17 May, the Meuse having been forced over a length of 20 kilometres, von Rundstedt's tanks poured into France. The Dutch surrendered, but the main strength of the BEF was yet to fully engage the Germans. Early on Thursday 16 May, the decision was made to withdraw the forward units of the BEF to defensive positions along the Escaut River. As the withdrawal began that night, Long made what was to be his last visit to the line. The press corps was ordered to move back to Arras and then Amiens. He reported optimistically that evening that the line was 'still holding firm', yet each day was marked by retreat. The journalists travelled by night 'on roads that were being mined and prepared to be blocked by carts against the German tanks that were at large over a wide area'. Soon holed up in Amiens, he reported that 'the Grand Hotel was hit and it was impossible to avoid the conviction that, as in Poland, the German bombers circled over the larger cities in which important staffs were living, singling out the right hotels with the deliberateness of a dentist extracting a tooth'.[6]

By early morning on 17 May, Lord Gort was faced with a grave situation. The French reported they were engaging ten German divisions. The enemy breakthrough now posed an imminent threat to rear General Headquarters, communications and base areas. Brigades were moved up to meet and delay multiple German advances to allow for the steady withdrawal of the main forces. By the end of the day, orders were issued for all administrative troops, including correspondents, to fall back immediately. Before dawn on Saturday 18 May, the members of the press corps were roused and instructed to move immediately back to the Channel Coast. Carrying only minimal hand luggage, Long and his compatriots travelled north via Abbeyville to Boulogne. This was a dangerous time for combatants and non-combatants alike. 'The enemy did not confine his attention to troops', he reported, 'but attacked the long columns of refugees that continued to move westwards'.[7] He began to file copy from Boulogne, citing his location as 'a Channel Port'.

The next day, as part of the preparations for the defence of Arras, all troops not required for defence were moved back in two echelons to Hazebrouck and Boulogne. Gort estimated that five German armoured divisions were about to break through to the coast and ordered plans be drawn up for the withdrawal of the BEF at Dunkirk. Long wrote, 'The picture now was no longer that of a line temporarily bent or broken, but of a besieged fortress'. All telephone communications between Arras and Paris were cut. For several days, the press office teleprinter at Arras was the only link to London, but when this teleprinter was smashed, the only way to send despatches to London was by King's Messenger, who crossed the Channel daily by steamer.

By 20 May, with German armour now clearly heading down the valley of the Somme and making for the Channel Ports, British anti-aircraft defences were provided for Boulogne. Refugees continued to pour into the town. Long observed 'an immense mechanized evacuation. Tens of thousands of vehicles are on the move – trucks, tradesman's vans, private cars, furniture carriers and brewer's lorries are crowded with people, bedding and clothing.'[8]

From Boulogne, he reported how difficult it was to give a precise account of events, partly because it was impossible to know exactly what was happening and partly because he was forced to valiantly dash out copy from his portable typewriter as 'every half hour or so, a flight of German bombers arrives here. Our machine guns spray their tracer bullets skyward. Heavier guns thump and pom-poms send their shells racing along the track of searchlights. Then comes the thump of bombs and the rooms shake.'[9] Lord Gort, overseeing an increasingly desperate rearguard action, and with the German tanks a mere nine miles from the Channel Coast and closing rapidly, ordered any and all 'useless mouths' to be evacuated.

At dawn on Tuesday 21 May 1940, Long and about 30 of his English, American and Dominion press colleagues – correspondents, broadcasters and photographers – were roused and ordered to board transports immediately for return to England. Hurriedly gathering their meagre belongings, they made their way past bombed buildings and wrecked vehicles down to the docks. There they joined a gathering throng of non-combatants, watchful for the first wave of German dive bombers to arrive for that day. A detachment of Royal Marines directed their embarkation on ships. Throughout the next two days, an increasingly harried evacuation continued under heavy aerial and artillery bombardment. Boulogne was completely overrun by the morning of the 25 May. Operation Dynamo was then activated – the epic evacuation of Allied troops from the beaches of Dunkirk.

As the press corps boarded their ship at Boulogne, Jocelyn Long was returning to Beckenham. Like most Britons, she relied on the newspapers and wireless bulletins for news and was therefore unaware that events across the Channel had deteriorated so rapidly. Civilians knew that battles were raging and that French, Dutch, Belgian and British forces were countering powerful German attacks; but what they did not yet know – what came as such a shock to them and to the world – was the spectacular success the Germans achieved that week in pushing the Allies back to the Channel Coast.

On 21 May, she returned home to be told that Gavin had telephoned from the *Herald* office in Fleet Street to let her know he was back in London. She had only received one brief letter from him since he'd left – the letter requesting the shoes. Now she was informed he was back!

In a letter to her mother a couple of weeks later, she described how she had dashed to board a train into the city to meet him:

> Mad with delight, I rang the office, found he was there sending off a message, so in I sped, pausing just long enough to tuck the children into bed. Gavin was talking on the telephone when I got in, and I peeped through the crack in the door to get an idea of the situation. He was looking Dreadful [sic] – lank and grey and concave, and hardly seemed to have energy enough to speak. I thought he might flop at any minute.[10]

As soon as he was free, she took him directly to a small eatery nearby and, with some food, revived him sufficiently for him to recount some of the events of the previous week.

A few days later, as the remnants of the BEF were being brought across the Channel, Long was sent to Dover to report on the arrivals. Such was the chaos of the time, the journey from central London, which normally took 40 minutes, took him five hours. Between 26 May and 4 June, over 300 000 troops arrived in England with little equipment and few weapons heavier than a rifle.

In the wake of Dunkirk, and as Australian troops began arriving in the United Kingdom for training, Long continued to report on the progress of the war as German air raids gathered momentum. In August he told his mother:

> I am glad that the children aren't at Beckenham. The Germans are shying any odd bombs they don't know what to do with at any railway line they come across. Number 71 [the boarding house in Albermarle Road where the Longs had been lodging] is just about the right distance away to collect a bomb, as they tend not to hit what they are aimed at.[11]

As it happened, he was right. In the months following, two high-explosive bombs did hit – one destroyed the nearby railway bridge and another demolished a house about 100 metres from their boarding house.

Gavin tried to keep his head down and do his job but, according to Gavin Souter, things at the *Herald* London office were 'in a state of considerable disarray'.[12] Staff tensions that had put Long in a difficult position since early 1939 had worsened. Souter relates that the strain of the blitz was beginning to tell on members of the staff. They were drinking considerably more than was good for them and personal relations were deteriorating. Long was frequently at loggerheads with editor Gordon Gilmour, who sacked one of his antagonists and asked Sydney to recall Long. Lou Leck, who managed the office, intervened on Long's behalf and Rupert Henderson responded by despatching Long to Libya and later Greece as correspondent with the Second AIF. The others were recalled to Australia.

In the meantime, Jocelyn and the children departed from Southampton for Sydney on the SS *Orcades* on 2 July. Soon after arrival, she wrote to Charles Bean, clearly anxious to reunite with Gavin:

> My problem is this. I have brought my children out from England and now am extremely anxious to return to Gavin. Apart from the moral aspect of the question (I have little or no right to want to go back and eat food that belongs to those who cannot leave the island), do you think it possible for me to get 1) permission, 2) a ship? And finally, 3) do you think I should abandon the idea as being purely selfish?[13]

From Dubbo on 19 September, Bean replied, offering to help procure a berth for her on a steamer, adding 'but … I feel certain that you ought to regard yourself as a soldier's wife – that is to say that the interest of the country should come first and, undoubtedly it is an advantage to get women and children and all extra mouths safely away from the old country'.[14] He pointed out the risks of a sea voyage and life in Britain and the grim wisdom of parents being separated in the event of harm coming to one or the other. He concluded, 'Please send your husband my love when you next write'. She chose to heed his advice and remained in Australia.

In October 1940, Long set sail for Egypt, arriving in time to report on the first Western Desert campaign. From 'somewhere at sea' on 1 November, he wrote to his mother:

> It has been a moderately uncomfortable voyage. No voyage can be very comfortable in war time in a blacked-out ship. I feel very isolated. The last letter from Jocelyn that reached me in London will be more than two months old by the time I reach my destination. I don't know what they are doing, but I hope they are living in Sydney and the children are going to school there. Jenifer will be a young woman before I see them again I fear. I wish I could have the day off and a magic carpet (we are going to the home of magic carpets) and arrive for the Christmas tree and the gathering of the clan.[15]

He then travelled with journalist Guy Harriott and a small contingent of officers from Alexandria to visit Jerusalem in late November. To his mother, he wrote: '[Jerusalem] is like an old, old relic wrapped in bright new cellophane. Outside the new Jews, the new architecture, pushful business methods, salesmanship, smart clothes, interior decoration, German conversation. Inside a little city which was probably very much the same when Pilate was its governor.'

In February 1941, after the momentous events of that winter for the Second AIF, Gavin met with his brother, Lindsay, known to all by his middle name, Merrick, who at that time was a sergeant commanding a platoon in the 2/3rd Battalion. Merrick was fresh from action at Bardia and Tobruk, after which he had been recommended for commission and a Military Medal 'for conspicuous gallantry'. Gavin and Merrick, nine years his junior, shared an enduring, mutual affection and respect. Long explained to Jocelyn in a letter:

> I got a lift along the road leading from Tobruk to the wadi where Merrick's battalion was resting. We both enjoyed having a long yarn from lunch until dusk. His men gave me a tin of stew and a tin of rice and we sat in his tent – made of Italian groundsheets – and he talked in his usual interesting and illuminating way. I have used a good deal of his talk for a series of articles which may be being used in the SMH.[16]

From North Africa, Merrick went on to serve in Greece, Syria and New Guinea before he was demobilised in October 1945 with the rank of captain.

On 2 March 1941, in a letter to his mother from Alexandria, Long lamented that he had been

> stuck here, doing practically nothing for a fortnight, and there may be some more of this enforced idleness before it ends. It was pleasant for a while, eating large meals, having regular baths, getting dirty clothes washed, letters written, but I am fed up with it now and would welcome a strenuous job to do.[17]

He described December, January and February as

> one long rush. There wasn't time to sleep or eat most days. There were such long distances to travel, often over broken roads or desert tracks. Always the greater part of one's time was spent, not collecting news and writing, but getting to and from the front, one's billet and the point where stories had to be delivered for transmission to Cairo.

He was beginning to feel the strain of long months of travel, isolation and strain. 'I'm war weary', he wrote. 'It is two years and three months since I last saw Australia, eight months since I last saw Jocelyn and the children. I would like a steady job, two days off a week, a home to live in and a hat on my head.'

He revealed to his mother that much of the first-hand information in the stories he had written about the battles of Bardia and Tobruk had been gleaned from his conversations with Merrick and that he hoped the *Sydney Morning Herald* had printed them. The *Herald* did publish a three-part series on 3, 4 and 5 March 1941 under the headline 'Campaign in Cyrenaica – The story of an A.I.F. platoon'. Gavin Long received the byline.

It wasn't long before a 'strenuous job' came his way. For the second time in less than a year, Gavin Long was about to experience an evacuation under fire, this time from Greece.

Italian forces had invaded Greece in October 1940 but had been driven back and held at bay by Greek and British forces near the Albanian border. By early 1941, Allied political and military leaders were divided on whether a force could be spared to assist Greece; but with a German invasion imminent and with Churchill very keen that a Balkan front be established, a commitment to send troops and supplies was agreed in March. Between 4 March and 3 April, Operation Lustre, comprising convoys designated 'W Force' and escorted by British and Australian warships, transported 58 364 Australian, New Zealand and British troops, 8588 motor transports, guns and tanks, as well as stores and other equipment from North Africa to Greece. Among the non-combatants were Australian pressmen Jack Hetherington, Reg Glennie, Chester Wilmot, Lawrence Cecil, Gavin Long and Ken Slessor, who embarked on HMS *Breconshire* on 24 March in the company of about 800 corps troops.

In a series of articles published in the *Brisbane Truth* the following year under the title 'The glory that is Greece', Lieutenant Colonel Eugene Gorman, Australian Comforts Fund Commissioner, recalled the non-combatants' experience:

> When the orders began circulating about embarkations for Greece, and as our names were on no nominal role, and no-one evinced any special desire for our company, we picked a nice large ship and picked well. Accommodation was scarce, so we tucked ourselves into a secluded spot on deck which served as a card room by day and a dormitory by night. Thus we reached Greece, so to speak, sea-going in a Lord Mayor's chariot. We disembarked at Piraeus and entered Greece oppressed by a sense of impending disaster. Five of us left Greece in the nautical equivalent of a garbage cart.[18]

Like many of the Australians and New Zealanders who had been transported to the olive groves and green fields of southern Greece in springtime, Long was enchanted by the country and its people, for whom he maintained a high regard ever after. On 5 April, he sent his son, Jeremy, a postcard from Athens with a cartoon depicting Mussolini being ground in a pepper mill by a Greek and a British soldier. The following day, the Germans invaded. By 20 April, after a series of Allied rearguard actions, the Greek Government agreed that 'W Force' should be evacuated.

The evacuation, Operation Demon, was ordered on 21 April. Long sent a report from Athens on the 23rd that was passed by the censor, cabled to Australia and published in the *Herald* the next day. He then joined 'some 1300 base troops, British civilians and 150 Germans captured at the Servia Pass [who] embarked in small Greek ships at Piraeus on the night of 23 April' to one of the dispersal areas at Nafplion, each large enough for about 1000 men and 150 vehicles. He was lucky to get out of

Piraeus that night. The following day, a similar embarkation, this time of hospital staff at Piraeus, ended in disaster with the large yacht Hellas bombed and sunk with the loss of almost all aboard.

At dawn on 24 April, Long joined thousands of men crowding the dock at Nafplion, awaiting their turn to board evacuation vessels. After dark on the 24th, he took his place among the groups of 50 who were marched along 'streets that had been bombed and machine-gunned that day and were strewn with glass' and began embarking at 10:30 pm on barges and ships' boats. By 3 am, almost 7000 had embarked for Crete. Gavin spent the next day in Crete, then he and Slessor embarked on the SS *Cherryleaf* with his kit and typewriter for the three-day voyage to Alexandria, arriving on the night of 27 April. He immediately sent off a cable to Jocelyn and then set about typing a report, which he despatched in the early hours of the 28th. It was published in the *Herald* on 30 April.

The previous day, Jocie had been enduring the all-too-common lot of service wives, trying to do their bit at home while fretting and hoping and praying about loved ones who had vanished in the fog of war. She was mightily relieved to receive the cable from Gavin that day. Australians had been reading daily newspaper stories about the terrible fighting in Greece and she had had no communication from him for weeks. 'My darling, my own', she wrote, 'WHAT a present from the telegraph boy. When your life is just a shell like this and you don't dare really think or feel at all you lose all sense of time. Now, under the influence of your weight-in-gold cable, I feel as if I've come out from an anaesthetic.'[19] She supplied news of the children and various friends, then described her exhaustion:

> Dearest one, reaction is settling in. I am so TIRED of all this. It's too long since this job started for you. How I wish the office would recall you for a holiday even – just a few weeks of home and normality. How tragic all this has been for you darling – to observe and not be able to do anything. Don't think that I fail to realise any of this because I don't talk about it – it's better that I shouldn't.

Then, on 30 April she received a letter he had written from Greece on the 10th, four days after the German invasion, affirming his love for her and reassuring her that he wished her to be happy with someone else in the future if he were killed. 'No woman ever got such a beautiful letter', she wrote. She then went on to declare that she had been unimpressed with his report published that same day in the *Herald*. 'I didn't at all approve of your message darling. It was much too technical and dry and detached for this kind of occasion.' She explained that journalist Ron Monson's story was 'splurged all over the front page of his paper' – the *Telegraph* – 'and rightly so, because it gave us public just what we want at the moment'. She declared that people at home were hungry, not just for the facts, but for 'personal stories, enthusiasm about the valour of the Anzacs. I'm always telling you to give us personal stuff.' She recalled how vividly Monson had described hitching a ride with a convoy of precariously loaded trucks, cautiously making their way along narrow, treacherous roads at night. 'Of course', she reproved, 'you couldn't have gone to Ron's lengths but something with LOCAL REMARKS. I don't a bit want to do this but you do ask for reactions so I'm being conscientious.' She appended a 'ps' to the letter: 'DO take my advice because I'm your public remember. I worship and adore you (though you probably don't think so).'[20]

On 2 May, still in Alexandria, he wrote a follow-up piece about the Greek campaign, which was published in the *Herald* three days later. It is one of the starkest examples of the journalistic hyperbole of which Long was often capable when describing Australians in battle, even when the sentiment was flatly contradicted by the outcome. Greece was lost, yet he praised two Australian battalions who had held up two German divisions at the Pineios River, exulting, 'No battle in the whole campaign showed so clearly that our men are simply too good for the Germans and completely lacking in respect for them and their methods'.[21]

Gavin Long was finally recalled to Australia, landing at Mascot on 10 June 1941, where he was eagerly met by his family. They had not seen him for almost a year. He continued his articles and editorials as defence correspondent for the *Herald* until 1943. However, the return to duties in Sydney did not go smoothly. Exhausted by the rigours and dangers of his journeys, he fell ill and was hospitalised for a couple of weeks with a debilitating skin infection. To make matters worse, he found it a challenge to adapt to the working and writing routine of a defence correspondent in Sydney, rather than a war correspondent near the battlefields. On 21 July, he expressed his frustration to his brother, Merrick:

> I am still more or less stuck at home with impetigo on my face and a beard full of ointment. It looks as if the stuff I want to write about army and naval matters is not quite the sort of nice reposeful stuff they want, and I will probably go to chief foreign sub-editor when I have got rid of my face in a few days.

During the next few months, his health slowly improved. He was able to maintain a steady routine as a defence writer, although there is evidence in a series of harshly critical diary entries he wrote that year and well into 1942 that he was mentally and physically exhausted.

He had returned to an Australia where people were struggling through a deepening war-weariness and a growing anxiety about their vulnerability to a southward advance of the Japanese. In his book *The Six Years War*, Long describes the mood in Australia throughout 1941 as one of 'impatience and irritation'. Newspapers, including the *Herald*, upbraided the government for not intensifying preparations for the defence of the country, while government ministers warned the people of the gravity of the situation and exhorted them to greater effort. It seemed everyone had an opinion about who to blame for the disastrous setbacks in Greece and Crete. German raiders were ranging throughout the Pacific and Indian oceans. The greater part of the AIF and the Australian Navy was fighting in the Middle East. The British and American focus was on the war in Europe and the Atlantic. The Australian militia was greatly expanded and put on full-time duty. Industry was harnessed to supply war materiel, and the 8th Division of the Second AIF, initially expected to join the 6th Division in the Middle East, had been held back in February in anticipation of a Japanese thrust.

In March, the British Chiefs of Staff informed Prime Minister Menzies that the threat from the Japanese was not considered sufficient to supply more air or sea power to the Far East at that time. The Americans preferred not to send warships to their base in the Philippines, believing that their main fleet would be safer in Hawaii, although American land forces and bombers were being established in the Philippines under General MacArthur by November. Very little air or sea power was available to defend the Malay Peninsula or Singapore. Britain provided two capital ships, HMS *Prince of Wales* and HMS *Repulse*, which arrived at Singapore on 2 December – less than a week before Japan opened hostilities with the United States by attacking the American fleet at Pearl Harbor and beginning their land and seaborne assaults southward.

The year 1942 began for Gavin Long with a two-week hospitalisation for appendicitis, after which he continued writing between four and 13 articles each month for the *Herald.* Of note was an admiring piece in June about the hard-won experience and professionalism of the returning Australian soldiers who had fought in the Middle East. This was a favourite theme of Long's and resulted in a lengthy commentary about what he called the 'standards of the AIF', by which he meant such things as 'merit-based promotion, businesslike efficiency' and respect deriving from being able to do a job well. He speculated that these standards were now being 'implanted throughout Australia as a whole'. It was Long's contention, and Bean agreed with him, that the Australian civilian population would inevitably imbibe aspects of exemplary character from the very presence of so many veteran AIF soldiers and that this would have a positive effect on nation-building. This contention arose from his overwhelmingly sanguine view of the Australian soldier and formed the foundation of his commitment to fostering education, especially of the young, about the history of Australians at war.

In April, Long was invited, as a representative of the *Herald*, to meet with John Curtin, who had been Australia's prime minister since October. Curtin, aware of the power of the press to influence public opinion, wanted to apprise the *Herald* of matters that he felt were important to Australia. Long made extensive notes and typed them into his journal later.[22] Curtin, clearly under great strain, described his grave fears about Australia's vulnerability to Japanese aggression and his frustration with Churchill's assessment that Australia was not seriously threatened. He believed that Churchill and Roosevelt underestimated the striking power of Japan. He recalled his years of frustration with Australia's unpreparedness for war despite all indications that one was imminent, and described many of the political, military and social complexities he, as prime minister, was dealing with daily.

Long spent the first two weeks of July in Port Moresby to report on the progress of the New Guinea Force, the blending of AIF and militia. His diaries reveal an unguarded, less charitable side to his character. He recorded in his diary that he was shocked by how bored and low-spirited the men were and he laid the blame for this directly at the feet of the officers – 'there are no bad soldiers, only bad officers' – who, after five months, had failed to keep the men busy with duties and drills or occupied with pastimes such as cinemas, clubs or activities. Long's personal notes reveal little patience or sympathy for indifference or incompetence, and little willingness to make allowances. He recorded scornfully, 'There are a lot of people around here who know fuck all about fuck nothing.'[23] In his articles in the *Herald* the following month, he was, naturally, more circumspect, acknowledging that two armies – men of the AIF and the militia – were experiencing the inevitable challenges of being welded together, but he observed that 'wise and enterprising commanders have proved that it can be done'.[24] Throughout this visit, and seemingly in anticipation of a future role as historian, he was collecting narratives from key soldiers. By 14 July, he was back in Townsville, and then on to Darwin, where he collected more personal narratives and generated reports for publication.

Like all newspapermen, Gavin Long was subject to the decisions of his editors. In August, he vented frustration about this in his diary: 'I have had no success in persuading the Editor to use a matter of fact article about the impracticability of trying to maintain a big force on the north side of the Owen Stanley Range. He has committed himself to being a member of the chorus demanding an offensive.'[25]

His frustration was also with what he regarded as the low quality of journalism in Australia at that time. He felt it was disappointing that, of a few dozen pressmen, the only ones who were submitting 'sound, explanatory, cool copy from the north' were Chester Wilmot and Osmar White. He described the problem as 'that of enlistments plus the sending of men overseas. Often the men who are doing the war reporting are second rate men who are writing over-coloured and misleading copy – writing, in fact, like English agency men.'[26]

Back in Sydney, Long was troubled by what he deemed 'gossip' in press reports of public drunkenness on the streets of Sydney and unruly behaviour on the part of returned soldiers and men on leave. Disturbed by these stories, he visited the Sydney central business area at night to find out for himself. Of about 500 men, presumably in uniform, he counted just three who were visibly drunk, describing them in his diary as merely 'wobbly'.

In a lengthy piece published in the *Herald* on 27 August entitled 'What AIF is thinking', Long turned the tables and reported not on opinions being expressed by civilians about soldiers, but what he had been hearing soldiers saying about civilians. 'In my experience', he began, 'a majority of the veterans who have come back are deeply disappointed by the talk and the conduct of the people, so much so that it is common to hear officers and men say that they are sorry they are here'.[27] He explained that the nub of the issue was ill-informed exhortations to action from the public when 'spirits are high' and recriminations broadcast far and wide when things are not going well. There was, in the opinion of many soldiers, 'too much criticism of the Army and its leaders'.

He believed that the soldiers who returned from Britain in the first year of the war had developed 'a glowing admiration for the coolness and stoicism of the British people during the intense German air bombardment', and that there appeared to be little of that in the Australian people, who seemed fearful and quick to complain. He proposed that the mood in Australia was understandable, given the widespread fear of invasion and sense of isolation as a European 'outpost'. He was moved by the words of an AIF commander, unnamed, he had heard calling on his men to bridge the divide between soldier and citizen whenever possible. 'We must set out', the officer had exhorted, 'each and all of us, like so many ambassadors, to trample on defeatism in all its forms. The public and inexperienced soldiers have an unconscious fear complex of the terrors of war. I want you to talk to these folk and do all you can to beat this fear complex.'

While generally praiseworthy about the Australian soldier and circumspect about Army leaders in his published articles, Long was nevertheless capable of scathing, ad hominem criticisms of senior officers in private. In a 1942 diary, he described a colonel as 'fat, uncommunicative and explosive', and mused on who would make a good commander-in-chief, dismissing various candidates as follows:

> Morshead, not big enough, bitterly critical of Staff Corps men; Lavarack, obstructionist, negative, failed in Armoured Division; Stantke, obstructionist; Cannan, a man obsessed by figures, an insurance company executive would be a better manager; Vasey, drinks; Allen, gets tight; Blamey, has made major mistakes and is capable of making more major mistakes; Rowell lacks decisiveness and experience.[28]

In September, feeling physically tired and professionally stagnant, he took the family on holiday. He returned on the 27th to an invitation to meet with Charles Bean at his Lindfield home. Bean had a proposition to put to him. Their conversation over the ensuing two days had an invigorating effect on Gavin Long, setting him on a new and challenging path that he would pursue energetically for two decades.

# 6
# BEFORE IT IS TOO LATE

*My final hope is that before it is too late (and it is fast becoming so) that there may be definitely selected, with eyes only on capacity and character, the architect who will be responsible for its* [the Official History of Australia in the War of 1914–1918] *perhaps greater sequel.*

– Charles Bean[1]

When Charles Bean met with Gavin Long in September 1942, he informed him of his intention to again petition the government to commission an official history of the war and for Long to be appointed as general editor. At that time, this plan had been almost a year in the making.

Largely at the instigation of Bean, a sub-committee of the War Cabinet had drafted a memorandum along these lines in October 1941 for discussion the following month. The committee comprised the chairman, Senator Joseph Collings (Minister for the Interior), Arthur Drakeford (Minister for Air and Civil Aviation), Frank Forde (Minister for the Army), William Ashley (Postmaster-General and Minister for Information) and Bean. After consultation with General Blamey, the committee recommended, among other things, that an official history be commissioned, that a start be made immediately on collecting materials necessary for the eventual history, and that the soon-to-retire Bean be replaced as soon as possible.

Cabinet was divided, both as to the timing of such a decision and the most suitable nominee. The *Telegraph* in Brisbane published that the selection of a general editor was between Bean's nominee, Gavin Long, Ian Fitchett (a distinguished war correspondent for Sydney's *Daily Telegraph*), Kenneth Slessor (journalist, poet and

Commonwealth Official War Correspondent) and Captain Frederick Howard (Melbourne journalist and historical records officer, Second AIF Corps Headquarters).

In reality, only Long and Slessor were serious contenders, although Slessor recorded in his diary, 'I still can't decide whether I really want it'.[2] However, the Cabinet deferred consideration of the scheme as 'premature'. The deferment was not primarily because of uncertainty about the candidates but because there was not yet any clear enthusiasm for the project itself. A few days later, the Japanese bombed Pearl Harbor and discussion of an official history was shelved.

Charles Bean's biographer, Peter Rees, notes that AWM Director, Colonel John Treloar, had a clear view on the inadvisability of approaching Kenneth Slessor for the role of general editor.[3] As well as his role at the AWM, Treloar was officer-in-charge of the Military History Section (MHS) at Army Headquarters, Melbourne. In that capacity, and in anticipation of the proposed official history, he had begun in 1941 to establish a collection of war records and relics. He was very keen for the Cabinet to make up its mind about an official historian and made no secret of his preference for Gavin Long. He discussed the two main contenders, Long and Slessor, with Bean. Treloar was not convinced that Slessor was the right man for the position. He wrote to Bean saying he thought Slessor was 'lazy' and had a 'wrong conception of his job as official correspondent'. He went further, complaining that Slessor 'had made no attempt to collect war records by interviewing the men as Bean did'. Treloar believed that Slessor had made no attempt to qualify himself for such a role. 'I believe Gavin Long is more solid and hard-working, and I think has a greater regard for exactness.'[4]

Bean also had reservations about Slessor, as did General Blamey; not that the decision rested with Blamey. '[Bean] was unlikely to hear anything positive about Blamey from Slessor,' Rees states, 'as the correspondent had become the commander's enemy through his reporting in the Middle East'.[5] Bean argued strongly for Long's appointment, never once expressing the slightest doubt about his suitability for the role. He cited Long's tireless patience, his understanding of warfare, his proven capacity to deal on a respectful yet equal footing with military and political leaders, and his ability to relate well to private soldiers.

Meanwhile, others were also concerned that work should begin as soon as possible. In July 1942, the Sydney-based Fellowship of Australian Writers wrote to Prime Minister Curtin, suggesting that the government 'should consider the possibility of commissioning a group of writers of established literary attainments to make a record' of wartime activities, both abroad and at home, encompassing both military and civilian endeavours.[6] The Fellowship felt that this project ought to be something more or other than ordinary war reporting or the generating of a 'factual historical record'. They envisaged capable writers being commissioned 'to move at will through all sections of the war services and to interpret what they see as they see it'. The writers would record and interpret events without censorship and with no expectation of publishing their writings immediately.

It is unclear what the Fellowship envisaged precisely – perhaps they imagined dramatised accounts based on real events, but they made no mention of Bean's official history as a model. Long, a member of the Fellowship, was aware of the suggestion and told Treloar that he felt it would be a good thing if possible, though he was concerned that censorship would be unavoidable. He recommended that Treloar meet with the Fellowship secretary as soon as possible to 'get down to something concrete'.[7] Incidentally, it is telling that, when approached to become a member of the Fellowship, Long's initial response had been, 'Do you think I'm eligible? Perhaps I should just be an associate member?'[8]

Cabinet considered the matter again on 4 August and this time approved the proposal as put by Bean the previous November. The AWM was to oversee the official history and the Cabinet sub-committee could nominate a general Editor. There was uncertainty about how much a project such as this would cost, so approval was given to spend up to 2000 pounds a year, even though nobody had a clear idea how many years it would take. Bean immediately approached Long, who agreed enthusiastically.

However, after the Board of Management of the Memorial recommended Long for the position in September 1942, it was again rejected by the War Cabinet in October. The problem was not Long's fitness for the role. The War Cabinet held a unanimously favourable opinion of him. The difficulty was, rather, that there was still an uneven enthusiasm for the project itself within Cabinet, particularly from an obdurate Ben Chifley, who had been sceptical of its value all along. But a personal memorandum soon after from Bean to Curtin had a decisive effect. On 25 November, unanimous approval was given to the proposal and the appointment of Gavin Long at a salary of 1500 pounds a year – the equivalent of a war pension available to civilians in government employment who had been injured on war service. On 30 January 1943, Senator Collings duly wrote to Long, offering him the appointment as 'General Editor and Editor of Records' of the official history.

In a conversation with Long a couple of months later, Chifley explained his earlier reluctance to agree to the history project.[9] He was keen to reassure Long that he had no hesitations about him personally, but that he was very concerned about the 'political aspects' of the official history, saying that a great part of the political context of what was decided was not set down in writing and would be unknown to future historians. How could a historian make sense of abbreviated Cabinet minutes, for example? It was rare for detailed notes to be kept of discussions and deliberations, he said, except by himself and a few others such as John Jensen (Secretary of the Munitions Department) and Frederick Shedden (Secretary of the Department of Defence, Australia's most influential public servant). And, ever sensitive to Commonwealth expenditure, Chifley also felt the first official history had cost too much. He was not a great admirer of Bean's history, except in an abstract sense. He thought it too long and thus unlikely to be widely read. He told Long that he preferred the idea of a 'potted history', something a busy man like him, who 'could not tackle a row of volumes', could take up and read.

In February 1943, Bean met Long and showed him the letter from Collings and the Cabinet minutes that recorded the decision to offer the appointment to him for an initial period of five years. The terms of the appointment made no mention of freedom from censorship. Bean agreed when Long declared that he would accept the position on two conditions: that he was not promising to complete the project in five years – his contract had to be renewed in 1948, 1950 and 1955 – and that he reserved the right 'to address the question of freedom from censorship after the war'. Long's contract called for him to prepare, in consultation with the AWM and the departments concerned, a provisional scheme for a history and, crucially, to recommend writers for the proposed volumes.

Gavin Long knew that a guarantee of freedom from official censorship would be essential to the credibility of the history. The bipartisan Advisory War Council agreed with this, and when the War Cabinet finally approved Long's plan, it promised that 'the exercise of censorship by the Government is to be limited to the prevention of disclosure of technical secrets of the three Services which it is necessary to preserve in the post-war period'.[10] Along with untrammelled access to official records, there was to be freedom of expression by the writers. In the preface to his first volume of the official history, *To Benghazi*, he was able to reassure his readers that the official history is not the government's version of history. Rather, 'this history is official in the sense that it has been financed by the Government, that the writers have been given access to official papers and have been conscious of the special responsibilities which rest upon writers of a national history'.[11]

Long's appointment as the general editor of Australia's official history was announced in February 1943. His erstwhile employer, *The Sydney Morning Herald*, proudly published the news, declaring that the government 'could have made no better selection from among the band of Press correspondents who have proved their mettle abroad with our fighting forces'.

Letters of congratulation began arriving immediately and a brief survey of the comments he received from friends and colleagues is illustrative of the esteem in which he was held by those who knew him well:

> 'I like the way you write the truth.' Lieutenant William Woodward, 1st Australian Armoured Division.

> '[I know that] matters will be considered in a truly impartial and analytical light thereby providing something of real value.' Colonel Robert Russell, Headquarters 2nd Australian Army.
>
> 'It has come to my attention that your war correspondent's credential and identification card has been surrendered. May I take this opportunity to express regret that your new duties have caused the termination of your accreditation. Our relations have been extremely pleasant and all who have worked with you regret that they are not to continue as intimately as they have in the past.' Colonel LeGrande Diller, US Army Public Relations, GHQ, Southwest Pacific.
>
> 'I've always hoped they would seize you for the job as I know of no one half so suitable. I gather the Army thinks the same way.' Noel Adams, war correspondent, *Advertiser.*
>
> 'Many of us here have been hoping that you would be appointed long ago.' Major-General Horace Robertson, 1st Australian Armoured Division.
>
> 'I write, as a past president of the Australian Journalists' Association to express the pleasure your appointment afforded me. This pleasure is shared by journalists in all parts of Australia.' Bob Perry, journalist, NSW Parliamentarian.
>
> 'You have the ability and the concentration and the style for such an undertaking.' Reverend George Cowie, Fullerton Memorial Presbyterian Church, Sydney.[12]

Long, emulating Bean, began keeping detailed diaries of conversations and observations while visiting Papua New Guinea as defence correspondent for the *Herald* throughout 1942, and now he started new diaries recording interviews, meetings and travel details. The diaries, currently held by the AWM, cover the years 1943 to 1959 and comprise

12 loose-leaf ring binders, each 100 or so typed pages with some handwritten sections in Long's neat, cramped style.[13]

On page 1 of the first diary, Long wrote: 'This diary, and others in the series, is written for the use of the authors of the Official History of Australia in the present war and is the property of the Commonwealth'.[14] In the diaries, he recorded conversations and impressions as seen by contemporaries because 'such impressions help to recapture the feeling of the period'. They also contain notes 'which consist of direct quotations from first-hand witnesses, generally about operations'. Long was careful to write notes while an informant was speaking or immediately afterwards. In addition to interviews, Long recorded observations of his own; for example, from an October 1943 visit to Townsville, 'There are far more AWAs and WAAFs in Townsville than there were when I was here last. Indeed there are as many women in uniform as men in the streets, and, among the men, a preponderance of Americans.' And, from Moresby that same month:

> The contrast between Moresby in July '42 when I was here last, and today, is most striking. In the early morning, the drone of aircraft is constant, unbroken for perhaps 20 minutes. Conversation is often interrupted during the day by the roar of aircraft overhead at low altitude – transports, bombers, fighters.' The contents of the diaries and Long's descriptions of them – what they contain, how he gathered them and why – demonstrate something of his careful, methodical manner. They also show the benefits, but also some of the limitations of beginning to gather material for a history while the conflict continued, rather than waiting until it was over.

He was quick to seek and receive advice from many quarters, some of it valuable, some specious. He was soon receiving a lot more advice than he actually asked for. In the first months, he fielded various opinions as to the purpose, scope and even desirability of the project and he heard many criticisms of Bean's official history. He recorded all of this in note form in the diaries, which provide clear evidence that he was actually listening to the opinions and criticisms offered and also, perhaps, for the benefit of a future biographer or historian.

First and foremost, Long sought out Charles Bean's advice. Years later he would report that Bean's advice 'was constantly obtained'.[15] This unusual phrase has suggested to some that Bean's constant advice was unsought or even unwelcome, that Bean was overbearing or interfering; but there is no indication in any of Long's writings that he was anything other than grateful. And such was the trust between the two men, and the character of each, that it proved to be a fruitful professional relationship.

Bean advised early that there should be an introductory volume of the new official history, 'chiefly an Army volume covering defence policy between 1920 and '39 and should include at least the Libyan campaign', and that the completed series should be more concise than the first history, with a more accessible, single-volume history being produced as soon as possible.

Early in 1943, Chifley, Long and Bean discussed a list of proposed volumes and content, including medical aspects, the role of women and escape stories by prisoners of war. To this end, very early on in the project, Bean suggested that Long talk with John Treloar 'about making sure prisoners of war (POWs) were adequately questioned from the historical point of view when they returned'. As it turned out, a volume focusing on POWs would never eventuate – a fact for which Long has been criticised. However, while no specific volume on POWs was produced, considerable efforts were made to incorporate their stories into the official history. Indeed, some 150 pages were given over to medical aspects of wartime captivity in the second volume of the medical series. Also, Albert Field, himself a prisoner of the Japanese from 1942 to 1945, contributed a comprehensive appendix to Chester Wilmot's volume *Tobruk and El Alamein*, entitled 'Prisoners of the Germans and Italians', and Lionel Wigmore, in his volume *The Japanese Thrust*, covered aspects of the experiences of Japanese POWs. Wigmore hoped his account would serve as 'a frame' into which individual published accounts of these experiences may, in time, be fitted. In his preface, Wigmore explained:

> Voluminous reports of the prisoner-of-war period were studied. Information drawn from these was checked with and supplemented by the large number of diaries kept by the prisoners, and by the many interviews collected by officers of the Repatriation of Allied Prisoners of War and Internees organisation, which are now systematically catalogued in the library of the Australian War Memorial. The thoroughness with which the interrogations were carried out at the end of the war made it possible for answers to be found from the prisoners themselves to almost every question which arose. These reports, diaries, and interviews have been plundered, sometimes without acknowledgment, with the object of providing an authentic account of the life of the Australians in captivity.[16]

In the early days of the history, as Long was developing his approach, he enquired of Bean whether he had found that it was best to make extracts from the papers of smaller units first and work from them to higher formations or vice versa. Bean said that he never resolved satisfactorily which was the best way to go and lamented that, only recently, an error had been uncovered in volume six of his history, which came about because 'he had decided to save time by not reading the diary of the brigade concerned'. Again and again, when he decided to disregard some source or other, Bean recalled that it had resulted in errors.

As for other advisers, there were many. Curtin counselled repeatedly that the official history should be 'popular', written with the qualities of 'journalese' and not too detailed. While individuals may want the stories of their own units included, most people would not read much detail. He reassured Long that the government was giving no directions, that it was vital there be no suspicion that the historian was partisan, and went on to say that all members of the Opposition had agreed that Long was the right man for the job. 'It seemed to me that the historian should be a layman's historian', Curtin said, 'presenting a broad picture. In the case of rationing, for example, it was more important what the citizen had on his plate than how the administration overcame its problem.'[17] He went on to say that the 'value of the last history was largely that it recorded accurately what happened to the men in the mud and not merely the broad staff picture'.

Long held John Curtin in high regard. This is clear in an observation he recorded after a lunch meeting with Prime Minister Robert Menzies in 1944. In his diary, he noted his opinion that Menzies 'was less egotistical than you would imagine', with 'a cultivated, but I still think, a lazy mind' and that 'the tortoise Curtin would not be outstripped by the hare Menzies on any course'.[18]

Treloar, as the Director of the AWM, notionally in charge of the implementation of the project under the Minister for the Interior, contended that the best way to write the history was to recruit suitable Army men who were present in engagements to write 'first narratives' as was the custom in the British Army and to submit these to the official history team of writers who would canvass other participants to make corrections. Long replied that he doubted the wisdom of the 'first narrative' method, stating, 'I have read a considerable number of diaries and was convinced of the need to obtain supplementary material, either by way of interview or in supplementary written narratives'. The danger with a 'first narrative', as he saw it, was 'that the readers to whom it was submitted would correct inaccuracies but not fill in the gaps'. He went on to cite the example of the diary of the 2/3rd Field Regiment in Greece that, although passed as 'correct', was 'brief to the point of being amusing, only supplying a few useful sentences to describe a most eventful 18 days'.[19] Bean agreed, adding that 'scrutiny of first narratives can become a kind of censorship'.[20]

In late 1943, with no end of the war in sight, Bean suggested that Gavin might begin drafting so-called 'Interim histories', an idea Long rejected. In a conversation with Treloar, he explained that he felt it would be wrong to attempt this as it was the task of military intelligence, as was the case in Britain. Treloar agreed, noting that the manuscript of a recent narrative from New Guinea submitted to Land Headquarters for publication in that year's Christmas book had been considerably altered by General Berryman to reduce the number of times General Vasey was mentioned and to insert two mentions of himself! Long saw this as a good example of the fact that 'interim history' is propaganda and had no place in an official history. Long suggested that Treloar should go ahead and publish the New Guinea narrative in *Khaki and Green*,[21] with a foreword noting that it had been 'read and revised by the general staff'.[22]

In a conversation demonstrating that Long was unafraid to stick to his guns in the face of contrary opinion, he disagreed with Treloar's stated opinion that a one-volume history would 'kill the sales of the longer history'.[23] Long argued that the risk should be taken. Treloar was unsure and recommended obtaining the advice of a publisher. He subsequently sought the advice of the Angus & Robertson publishing house, who bolstered Treloar's opinion that such a process would probably be disastrous for sales of the more detailed history to follow. Long argued against the publisher's advice, citing the nature of the buyers of the longer history, who would be motivated by their personal interest to have more detail than a single volume could provide. As it turned out, the single volume was not published until 1973, so the point remained moot.

Further unsolicited advice came from Brigadier Roy King, then commander of the 16th Brigade, who was cynical about war history in general. 'The truth about that show [the Greek campaign] will never be known', he said to Long, concluding, 'the trouble is there is so much bloody lying. You can't tell the truth about people in a war. People must be whitewashed. The object of reports is to make the writers appear in a good light.'[24] We do not have Long's response to this opinion, but he did take the trouble to record it in his diaries – proof that he was all the while listening and honing his judgment about such matters.

He also heard many freely expressed opinions about Bean and his history of the war of 1914–18, many of them critical. He routinely passed on these criticisms to Bean, who often agreed with them in principle, if not always in substance. In March 1943, Attorney-General HV 'Doc' Evatt complained vaguely that Bean did not write the history 'in the right way'.[25] Blamey was sceptical that anyone could be found who would have the ability to do a history of the current war and was especially critical of Bean's effort, asserting that it 'had not been well done'.[26] He suggested that the British War Office history had been done better, while Bean's was an accumulation of unit histories and was too detailed. He concluded that Bean had set out to say how things should have been done without being qualified to do so.

Long defended Bean by arguing that the achievements of the relatively small AIF could only be appreciated if their stories had been told in great detail. When he told Blamey that he was planning to go north with the troops as soon as the scheme for the history had been finalised, Blamey was not encouraging, claiming that Bean in the last war had a compact force to cover and spent too much time chasing detail. Blamey asked about how Long intended to incorporate 'the politics'. Long replied that he would follow the example of Bean and 'trace the events right from the Cabinet room to the front line'. Blamey further contended that much of importance would never be accessible. Long replied that in the last war, all documents had been made available, but Blamey doubted that this would be the case regarding the present war.

General John Northcott, Chief of the General Staff, repeated to Long the frequently heard criticism that Bean's history was too detailed and did not bring out tactical lessons.[27] Long replied that, even if this were true, it was an accurate narrative and a basis for any writer of tactical and technical studies. Northcott wondered whether it was even accurate. He felt that senior commanders ought to be consulted rather than junior officers. Long said that the method he would adopt – as did Bean – was to see the picture from the senior commander's standpoint and then to proceed down to company and platoon. In November 1943, while Long was visiting New Guinea as the *Herald*'s defence correspondent, Blamey once again complained to him about Bean, criticising his history for being 'full of trivia ... destined to gather dust on shelves and never be read'.[28] He repeated that Bean had criticised tactics and strategies when he wasn't qualified to do so, and he was unbalanced in his treatment of individuals. Long countered that returned soldiers read Bean's history, with about 20 000 copies of the final volume having been sold at the time. Blamey then admitted to not having read very much of it, but was merely reporting what others had told him about how Bean 'has made awful blues here and there'.

Back in Sydney, Long put these criticisms to Bean, particularly that his history had been too detailed. In response, Bean cited a conversation with John Gellibrand, his own mentor and an officer Bean greatly admired, who told him that, as a junior officer, he had sought to read whatever he could find about what actually happened to a soldier in battle.[29] This influenced Bean to determine to write of 'the feelings of the men' and 'the experiences of the soldier'. While there may be legitimate criticisms, said Bean, how else to convey the truth of a matter without detailed, supporting evidence?

Long took the trouble to note down further criticisms of Bean from John Jensen (Secretary of the Department of Munitions), Arthur Drakeford (Air Minister) and General Vernon Sturdee who quipped that, in Bean's history, 'every lance-corporal gets a mention!'[30] In fact, 363 of the 2267 participants Bean named in volumes two and four of his history were privates (or equivalent), lance-corporals or corporals – about one-sixth of all those who 'get a mention'. By contrast, in the three volumes Long wrote in his history, these ranks account for about one-fifth of the total (415 of 1889).

There were many, however, who were quick to praise Bean's history and hold it up as a model. General Henry Wynter, in charge of administration at Land Headquarters in Melbourne, said that he thought Bean's history had been well written. Long held Wynter in high regard, calling him 'perhaps the clearest and most profound thinker the Australian Army of his generation has produced'. While interviewing troops in Atherton, North Queensland, Long asked Brigadier Rogers, then Director of Military Intelligence – the senior intelligence officer in the Australian armed forces and veteran of Middle East campaigns – for his opinion.[31] Rogers said he had read all of Bean's history and thought it was 'a great piece of work'. He added that he was aware that some senior officers were unhappy that Bean had expressed opinions about leadership in the AIF and that the detail was too great. He, however, had seen Bean at work in the trenches at Helles and 'knew how carefully he worked and believed that it was necessary to work that way to discover the truth'. Long was told by the United States Army historical officer, when visiting Humboldt Bay, that the 'American plan for a war history now included conducting a short course for historical officers. Bean's was held up as "the model" of what a war history should be.'[32]

Throughout 1943, 1944 and 1945, as he was drafting a plan for the history, Long continued to energetically gather reports and documents, interviewing potential writers and drafting chapters. He was surely aware that he had committed himself to an enormous task, and yet it was not until many years later that he would look back and confess his naivety. 'I didn't know when I started', he reflected, 'how unfitted I was for the job. I went into it with a fairly light heart and great enthusiasm. It wasn't long before my temerity began to appal me.'[33]

Second row, centre: Gavin Merrick Long and Herbert Edward Britten.
Macarthur House, The King's School, Parramatta, c. 1922/23. *Long family papers*

'This is a rickshaw in which you can joggle along the streets of Singapore Dad.' Postcard from Gavin to son Jeremy, Singapore, 11 April 1938. *Long family papers*

'Dearest Jen, this is one of the most enchanting click pictures by Van Gogh I have ever seen. Do you remember the Van Gogh picture we had at Suttie Road with the woggly postman in it. The BBC announced your safe arrival in Melbourne. You must be rather important. Dad.' Postcard from Gavin to daughter Jenifer, London, 17 August 1940. *Long family papers*

War correspondents prepare to embark for Greece. Reginald Glennie, John Hetherington, Gavin Long, Ian Fitchett, Maslyn Williams and Kenneth Slessor. Ikingi Maryut, Egypt, 23 March 1941. *AWM 006819*

War correspondents. (L to R) Reg Glennie, Chester Wilmot, Gavin Long, Captain Eric H Wilson and John Hetherington. Near Lakoudi, c. April 1941. *AWM 007820*

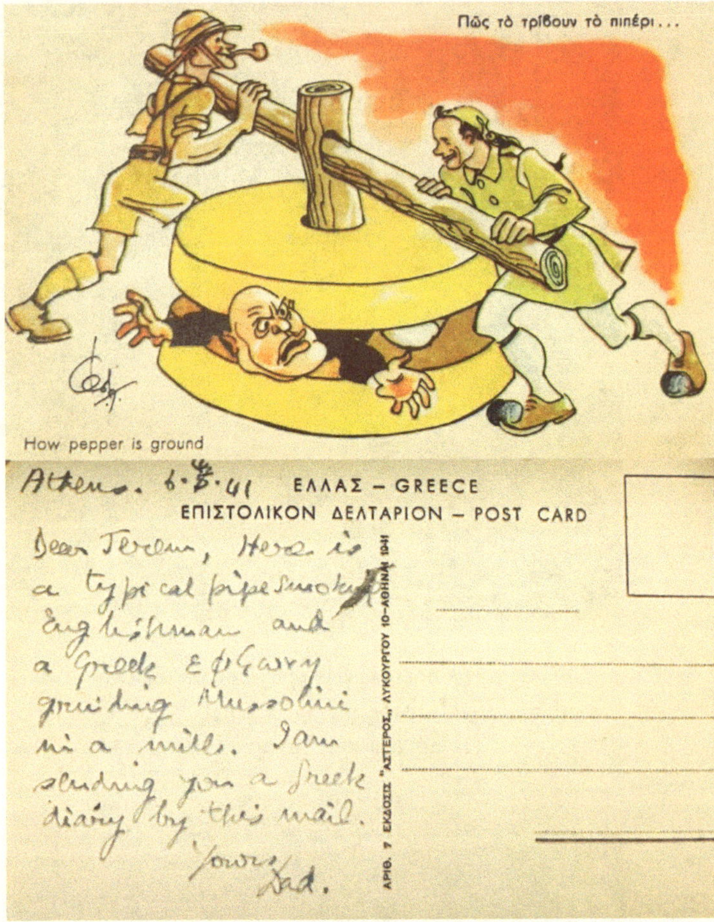


'Dear Jerem, here is a typical pipe smoking Englishman & a Greek grinding Mussolini in a mill. I am sending you a Greek diary by this mail. Yours Dad.' Postcard from Gavin to son Jeremy, Athens, 6 April 1941. *Long family papers*

Gavin Long's note on rear of photo: 'War reporter cross questions pompous German Squadron Leader. On SS "Helen" on way to Crete.' c. April 1941. *Long family papers*

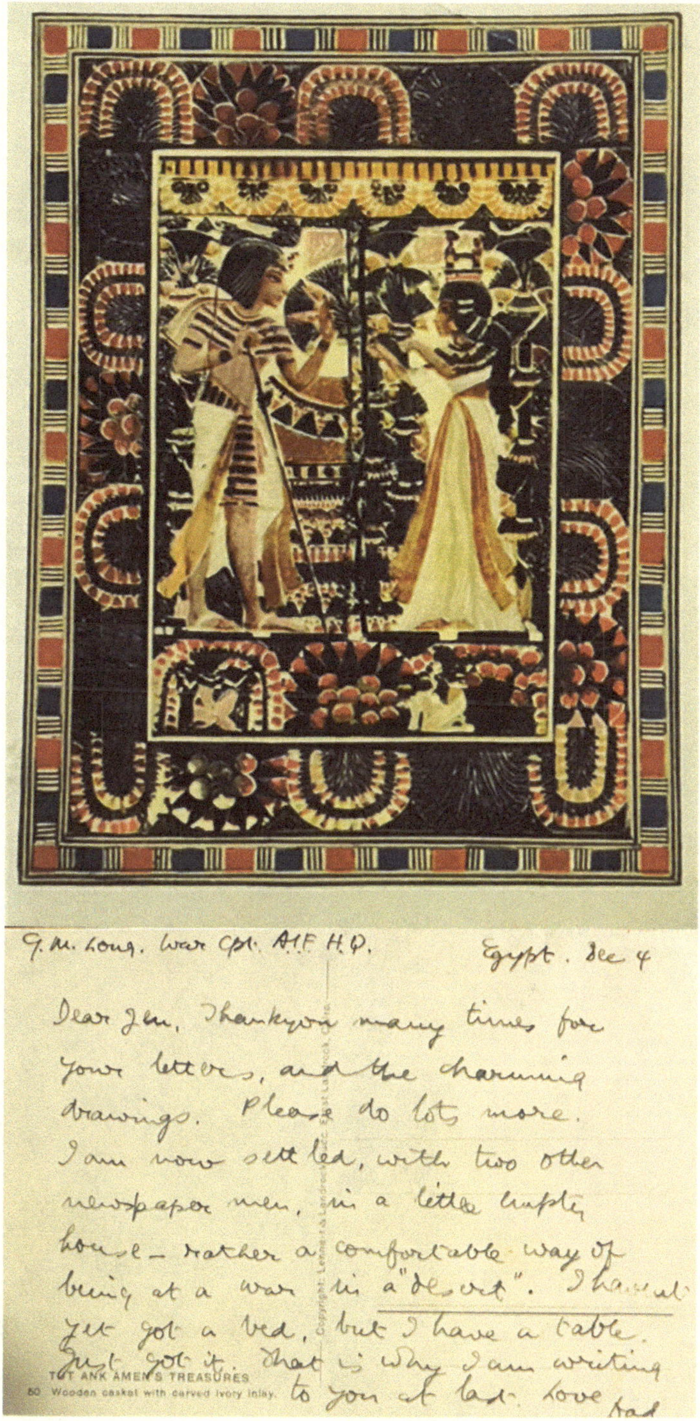
G. M. Long. War Cpl. A.I.F. H.Q. Egypt. Dec 4

Dear Jen, Thankyou many times for your letters, and the charming drawings. Please do lots more. I am now settled, with two other newspaper men, in a little empty house – rather a comfortable way of being at a war in a "desert". I haven't yet got a bed, but I have a table. Just got it. That is why I am writing to you at last. Love Dad



'Dear Jen, thank you many times for your letters and the charming drawings. Please do lots more. I am now settled, with two other newspapermen, in a little empty house – rather a comfortable way of being at war in a "desert". I haven't yet got a bed, but I have a table. Just got it. That is why I am writing to you at last. Love Dad.' Postcard from Gavin to daughter Jenifer, Egypt, 4 December 1941. *Long family papers*

Frank Bagnall and Norman Brown, enjoying a meal break with Gavin Long. Sattelberg track, 6 December 1943.
*AWM 016252*

Gavin Long and Charles Bean.
*AWM 129035*

Writers' meeting. (L to R): (back) D Gillison, L Wigmore, G Hermon Gill, A Walker, C Wilmot; (centre): P Hasluck, S Butlin, G Odgers, J Herington, D Dexter; (front): J Balfour, D Mellor, G Long, D McCarthy. Acton, ACT, 1954. *AWM 044512*

Writers' meeting. (L to R): G Long, C Wilmot, A Walker, P Hasluck, L Wigmore, G Odgers, J Herington, S Butlin, D Gillison, G Hermon Gill, D Mellor, D McCarthy, D Dexter, J Balfour. Acton, ACT, 1954. *AWM 044513*

Gold Cross of the Royal Order of the Phoenix awarded to Gavin Long in 1956 for his contribution to promoting Greece's stature abroad.
*AWM REL33435*

Bronze bust of Gavin Long by John Stuart Dowie, 1970. This bust, alongside that of C.E.W. Bean once flanked the main entrance of the Australian War Memorial and is now in storage.
*AWM ART27671*

# 7
# A TRUE AND FAITHFUL RECORD

*The aim of the history, it was agreed, was to tell the story as a human experience; not primarily to teach the lessons of war.*

– Gavin Long[1]

Poised to begin the biggest undertaking of his professional life in March 1943, Gavin Long replied to the many congratulatory letters he had received. One of these, noted earlier, was from Major General Horace Robertson.[2] He acknowledged Robertson's observation that 'some organising will have to be done to catch up the time that has been lost' because the project was getting underway without the voluminous notes that Bean had already acquired at the time the first official history got underway. 'My first job after I leave the *Herald* this week', he optimistically declared, 'is to see the Ministers and departmental people concerned, and then, with the board of the Australian War Memorial, help to plan a history. This will probably take some weeks.' As it turned out, the final draft of his plan would not be approved by Cabinet until November 1945. The delay was caused by wartime demands on Cabinet decisions rather than by any sluggishness on Long's part. He continued, 'When that is done I can get down to detail. I would like to go to New Guinea as soon as I can, also talk to units recently there, with the object of adding to the records of the Owen Stanley-Buna campaign.'

He then spent a day with Bean, discussing the provisional scheme to be submitted to the government as soon as possible. Bean recommended that the submission should start with a discussion of the previous history, drawing on lessons learned from its production. Both men agreed that the new history 'must carry the proof as well as the assertion' and the proof could only be achieved by rigorous attention to detail.[3] They both felt that a short, popular history under 500 pages should be published quickly, then the larger, more in-depth volumes. No short, popular history of the previous war had been written because of the reluctance to publish such a history in the face of widespread anti-war sentiment after 1918. They believed that such objections no longer prevailed in Australia and that the absence of such a volume had meant that 'for a generation, school children and teachers were very slightly informed about the history of the Australian forces and people in the last war'.[4] Bean's one volume, *Anzac to Amiens: A Shorter History of the Australian Fighting Services in the First World War* would not eventuate until 1946. As it turned out, the new history was to prove so demanding through the next two decades that the proposed volume, *The Six Years War – A Concise History of Australia in the 1939–1945 War*, was destined to be Gavin Long's final project and he would not complete its final draft until just before his death in 1968.

At this 1943 meeting, the two men also began canvassing the names of potential writers. Indeed, the selection of writers was to prove a protracted and difficult business for years to come.

A few days after meeting with Bean, Long travelled to Canberra to discuss with Arthur Bazley, AWM acting director between 1942 and 1946 and a member of the War Archives Committee, how to begin gathering raw material from thousands of participants in hundreds of campaigns across the globe. Bazley showed him around the AWM library and they discussed who to begin interviewing. While he was there, he saw Frank Thorpe, the Public Service Commissioner, about salaries for writers and staff, then met with Colonel Arthur Butler, author of the three-volume *Official History of the Australian Army Medical Services in the War of 1914–18*. He then went to Melbourne to begin drafting his grand scheme for the history.

The energy Gavin Long expended throughout 1943 is staggering. In the 80 days between 4 March (his first full day on the job) and 23 May, he travelled back and forth between Canberra, Melbourne and Sydney, sometimes by air, often by train, conducting and recording no fewer than 70 meetings with 58 people. His conversations with them covered such topics as how best to gather and preserve records, how to establish history units for each service, and how best to gain access to serving officers and men of other ranks. He gathered dozens of suggestions about who might be approached to write the volumes, what issues should be covered in the history and in how much detail, and how to consult and establish co-operative efforts with agencies and foreign governments in drawing together documents and records to underpin a credible narrative. He sought advice from senior public servants in various departments related to the war effort, including Defence Secretary Frederick Shedden and Commonwealth Prices Commissioner Douglas Copland; senior officers in all three services, including General Blamey; government heads, including Prime Minister Curtin, Treasurer Ben Chifley, Minister for External Affairs HV Evatt, Minister for the Interior, Senator Joseph Collings, and Minister for Aircraft Production, Senator Don Cameron; and two others who would eventually be commissioned as writers – Chester Wilmot and G Hermon Gill. He then consolidated his impressions from these interviews under the guidance and mentorship of Bean and the direction of AWM Director John Treloar, at that time in Melbourne on secondment to the Army.

By April, he had prepared his first draft plan and typed it up. In it, he specified the scheme's aim: 'To crystallise the facts once and for all for any subsequent use, to establish a story that would carry conviction in other countries and to satisfy the men and women who took part that the history was a true and adequate memorial of their efforts and sacrifice'. This stated aim remains the basis on which the official history may be judged.

On Bean's advice, he travelled to Melbourne to discuss this draft with Treloar, who recommended getting approval for the plan from the War Memorial Board. Long submitted the plan to the Board at the beginning of May 1943 with the hope of a unanimous agreement, thereby removing the need for a meeting. Several members expressed concerns about the length and complexity of the series, so a meeting was called for the 24th. While waiting, Long flew back and forth between Melbourne and Sydney, continuing his research and beginning to arrange for a badge and pass to travel to General MacArthur's headquarters in Brisbane. Long was anxious to secure the release of documentation relating to recently completed American operations in the Southwest Pacific, none of which were being made available at that time because of MacArthur's insistence on secrecy. On the advice of Shedden, he drafted a letter for the prime minister's signature, explaining his task and requesting a meeting with the general.

On 26 May, Long was relieved to hear that the War Memorial Board had approved his plan. He and Bean prepared notes to guide Senator Collings in presenting the plan to the War Cabinet three weeks later. Long was called into the meeting to answer questions. It was then that the months of thought, advice and preparation paid off. According to his detailed notes of the meeting, he deftly and confidently responded to various questions and doubts expressed by the powerful and opinionated Cabinet members.

At the meeting, there was considerable discussion about remuneration rates for writers.[5] Long had proposed 1500 pounds per volume. When Curtin asked, 'Is that not a large fee?', he explained that it would be necessary for the writers to make this a full-time job, giving up employment elsewhere for at least a year. Persisting, and displaying considerable naivety, Curtin then wondered if most of the material for the volume would not already have been provided for the writer. 'I can imagine', he suggested, 'a writer writing for a month while the mood is on him, and again during a vacation, and getting it done'. Long explained that much material would indeed be provided for the service volumes by the historical sections of the services, but not for the civilian volumes, and that considerable travel may be demanded of writers, including time in Canberra.

Then came a discussion about whether war correspondents would be the best writers. Long acknowledged that he did have some in mind, prompting some less-than-flattering comments from both Chifley and Curtin about the opinions expressed by correspondents in their newspaper columns. Chifley offered that war correspondents had made predictions and been proved wrong. Long countered that war correspondents don't make predictions; they report events. Curtin politely reassured Long that he was not included in these criticisms, which was partly why he had been chosen, then returned to his opinion that there ought to be an introductory volume dedicated to general defence policy. Long had no hesitation in expressing disagreement, noting that Bean had made a similar suggestion. Long believed that such a volume would be less popular than one that included at least one campaign narrative, namely, the first campaign of the Army – at Bardia – which was the product of said policy. Chifley then asked, 'Who can write about defence or munition policy? The only men who could write would be men like Mr. Shedden and Mr. Jensen. They are the only men who know everything.' Long pointed out that 'the historian will have to rely on the recollections of such men'. Then Curtin got to what may have been his chief concern, asking, 'Who in the world can write cogently of general defence policy and also has knowledge of the first Libyan campaign?' Long replied diffidently, 'I'm afraid I intended to write that volume myself'.

Shedden, well aware that his own record on defence policy would form part of the published history, asserted that he was troubled that a survey of Australia's defence posture between 1920 and 1941, as proposed, would be an immense and fraught exercise with contradictory opinions to be canvassed. Long countered that the historian's job would be to gather and report such opinions, adding that he and Bean believed that the reader should be informed about what happened between the wars and thus it was vital for the historian to provide 'a link between the last official history and the new one'.

Curtin then wondered if the volume covering the Middle East campaigns couldn't be written immediately. Long answered: 'A good deal of work could be done on it during the war but the whole story cannot be told until we have the enemy side of it. And men who are now prisoners of war must come back and be interviewed. Whole units disappeared in Crete for example.'

At the conclusion of the discussion, Curtin said he wanted the Advisory War Council – the body comprising members of government and opposition that provided bipartisan advice – to approve the plan so that no political party could be perceived to be giving final direction. Then, still uneasy about committing to a specific stipend for the writers, but acquiescing to Long's point that something definite would need to be presented to prospective candidates, Curtin requested that the words 'about £1500' be minuted.

The Advisory War Council met on 16 June but deferred discussion of the history plan because Curtin was unable to attend due to illness. Impatient to go north to begin three months of interviews with General MacArthur's officers, personnel at the Advanced Land Headquarters in Brisbane and Australian 6th Division troops in North Queensland, Long gained Curtin's permission to absent himself from the next meeting and immediately began making travel plans, arranging for permissions and clearances. He arrived in Brisbane on 28 June and reported to the War Memorial branch office there. His observations while staying in Brisbane that week provide an insight into the wartime capital that was then hosting almost 100 000 Americans.

> In cafes and hotel dining rooms there are 20 US troops to every 10 Australians, and of the Australians only 2 or 3 are women. The troops want amusement, food and drink, consequently the National Hotel where I am staying is feeding three sittings each night. The bars are open generally only from 5 to 6. I have seen none open on Saturday afternoon. Cigarettes, bottled liquor and matches are unprocurable in the shops and hotels except by the favoured customer. The cafes are short not only of staff but of equipment. Many US cigarettes and matches circulate and this blunts the edge of the shortage. As in the south, it is noticeable that the civilian girls who go out to dinner with US officers are generally not 'ladies' – not of the class that would normally eat at the better hotels. The girls in uniform are almost invariably with Australians.[6]

On 8 July, while Long was visiting training camps and staff headquarters in and around Brisbane, taking copious notes from interviews with more than 100 people, the Advisory War Council met and endorsed Cabinet's approval of his provisional plan, subject to agreement about the names of the writers and providing that the volume on defence policy was not to begin until a later time. However, it was not until five weeks later, on 16 August, that Long heard the news that the plan had been approved. He had been working in the Atherton army training area, ignorant of the fact. 'If I had received this news earlier', he noted in his diary with some annoyance, 'I would have gone south to begin writing to proposed writers'. Despite this, he felt confident that he had at least gathered some very valuable material and 'felt better qualified to meet the next problems'.[7]

The approved plan, which was to undergo several revisions, provided for the writing of 16 volumes in addition to those for a medical history that was to be prepared by an editor nominated by the medical directors-general of the three services. Federal government departments would be responsible for the documentation of wartime departmental histories, not necessarily for publication. A naval historical records section was to be established and the Air Force historical records section would be enlarged. Cabinet approved a revised plan in November 1945, and this was again amended in 1950. In the revised plan in the civilian series, there would be two volumes on government and the war's effect on the people, two on economic developments and one on wartime science and technology. After consideration, Long decided there would be no volume describing the combined operations of the three services. He felt they were so seldom in action together that separate volumes devoted to each service would suffice.

The plan, or 'scheme', that Long had proposed arose from his convictions about the nature and purpose of an official history. In semi-regular circular letters to his writers over the next few years, through which he offered resources to assist and encourage them and ensure consistency in their volumes, he drew on international examples – from Britain and New Zealand – when describing the nature and purpose of the official history as he saw it. He referred them to guidelines provided to writers of the British history by Cambridge professor and editor of the military series of the British official history Professor James Butler in 1948.[8] He noted that Butler had emphasised the importance of recognising that an official history does not set out the official view of the government. That would be propaganda. The views expressed by the writers of the official history were their own. Writers retained independent judgment as historians, based on their research into all available sources, and they would bear the responsibility for what they wrote.

He explained that the imagined readers of the history would include professional students of war who wanted to have an accurate and comprehensive account of the conduct of a war, public servants who form and guide national policy, and educated general readers. 'It will not be our function', Long reminded his writers, 'to present our own opinions as the morals which ought to be drawn. We shall try to let the facts suggest their own conclusions.'

In a 1950 circular letter, he quoted General Howard Kippenberger, then editor-in-chief of the New Zealand official history.[9] Kippenberger had lamented what he perceived as 'widespread ignorance' in New Zealand about the 1914–18 war, which, in part, led to New Zealanders being 'blind and unready in 1939'. Kippenberger had declared

> it is our duty and our ambition to prepare and set before the people of this country and the world, a true and faithful record of what was done and suffered, endeavoured and endured and accomplished by New Zealand and New Zealanders in the gravest years of our history, without fear or favour, without malice or concealment.

Reflecting on the project years later, AJ Sweeting recalled that Gavin Long's goal was to observe and record for posterity, with great attention to accuracy and detail, the course of the entire world war and Australia's involvement in it, beginning well before the conflict began in 1939.[10] Sweeting remembered that Long sought to devise and oversee 'a means of bringing the history of those events into a coherent, well-proportioned whole', providing leadership and guidance to his team of writers whose volumes would contain some seven million words – 'by far the largest Australian literary project undertaken up to that time'. It was his responsibility, as general editor, not only to produce his own volumes but to ensure that his writers, researchers and staff worked as teams to produce a unified, integrated series that was credible, worthy and ultimately saleable; that is, as appealing to a broad readership as possible.

Through 1944, Long continued to refine plans and canvass potential writers. In May, he recorded his impatience with delays.[11] In his diary, he wrote:

> Five months have passed since I left Sydney for Canberra on January 1st, intending to have outstanding work there and in Melbourne cleared by the end of February and return to Atherton or New Guinea to visit Americans and do a month's work with 21 and 25 Brigades on Syria.

Yet his achievements in this period of frustrating delays were impressive. They included: helping to establish the Royal Australian Air Force (RAAF) historical section, producing a circular on departmental histories, securing the Memorial's approval of medical historian Dr Allan Walker, defining the duties of staff who were yet to be appointed and gathering about 40 000 words of historical notes. He spent a total of 29 exhausting weeks between October 1943 and September 1945 travelling to the locations of Southwest Pacific campaigns – New Guinea, the Solomon Islands and Borneo.

While in Port Moresby at the correspondents' camp at New Guinea Force Headquarters, Long interviewed staff officers and reporters, seeking suggestions about potential writers for the history, as well as acquainting himself with operations. He was frequently quite close to danger. At Finschhafen, for example, he watched Japanese bombers dropping phosphorous and high-explosive bombs, and later came under fire from Japanese 75 mm guns while observing from an American patrol torpedo boat.

A few letters from Gavin to Jocelyn have survived from this time, as well as postcards he sent to the children. Though brief, the letters were newsy and frequently punctuated with wry humour. Gavin was aware that while Jocelyn was being the stoical, brave wartime wife and mother, she constantly fretted about his well-being. Eager to reassure her and ever self-deprecating, he would regale her with humorous anecdotes and descriptions of life from army encampments in the islands. His letters offer a glimpse into their close and often playful relationship. At that time, the Longs were living in Bellevue Hill in Sydney and there is no doubt the postman was as eagerly anticipated there as in countless other homes across wartime Australia.

On 29 July 1944, Gavin wrote:

> Darling, Back again at N.G.F. [New Guinea Force] after 3 days of travelling including a torrid night in the bowels of an American LCI (Landing Craft Infantry) and a fair share of 'strip sitting'. This term is best described by mentioning that in every Movement Control office you will surely see a print (comic strip) of an overburdened troop presenting himself at a hut marked Movement Control and nearby are 3 men, one a skeleton, one nearly so and the third only skin and bone. The legend is: 'You'll have to wait a while. Join those men over there.' That took longer to tell than it was worth. I wrote little to you from the Madang area simply because I was able to work so hard, plus the paucity of the light at night. On my return 12 letters from you were waiting. I've lost my precious scissors, my hat and my shaving brush. The cad who has been occupying this hut has eaten all my barley sugar. It should be pleasant on this next tour. A number of the senior blokes are friends and have pressed me to come. Sorry to be so uninformative, but as I've chiefly been living at h.q. this trip, to mention names or places is to give away the whole picture. More tomorrow darling. I will post with this a letter written earlier but not posted because I was sure it would be quicker to carry it part of its way myself. Love, G.[12]

On 24 January 1945, he described a typically arduous journey, the long hours, uncomfortable air and sea transport, and he illustrated his letter with comical ink drawings. They depicted a man sleeping on a floor, then sitting on boxes, then resting in a recliner. He also described snacking on American doughnuts and coffee, then

> lunch at an Aussie staging camp, but by then we'd lost our gift for eating. I have a tent on my own and no sign of a sharer yet. Bill has a cold caught in the plane. He had a sweater but I had a sweater and that raincoat and was glad of its weight. Bitter pill – tons of fags here – no limit and of course they are so soggy there's little pleasure in smoking. I hope you began writing as soon as I left. If so, I should get a letter any day now. Dermatitis rife because of the damp climate. I hope I don't get caught in this way. It would be most galling. There are so many small things that can bring one so low in these parts.

On 13 February, he wrote from Bougainville, expressing concern for her health as she was briefly in hospital. He acknowledged a 'sweet letter from Jen' and promised to reply to her 'ere long'. He apologised for the brevity of his letters, explaining that 'the detailed notes I write in my little black books mitigate against letter writing'. Then he followed with a lovely description of a recent event:

> I arrived here a fortnight ago. Last night I sat on the beach and listened to a gramophone concert. An extravagantly lovely sunset over the smooth sea. As the Bolero tum-tummed the waves hush-hushed, smacked and flopped on the grey sand. A landing barge that had been lying idly off shore, black against the sunset, stirred and turned slowly and glided, like a protruding sea monster to the shore, slapped its ramp on the wet sand. It had come to the concert.
>
> I am very happy to find that I am very fit and battling well, which is very encouraging after my poorliness during the last few months in Australia. If all is well (touch wood) I'd like to spend a week when I get back cleaning up routine jobs with Bill [Sweeting] and then take 14 days leave with you. I'm very fit. A bit tired. Sent the kids some postcards as a substitute for letters to you.

On 29 March from a Field Ambulance station, he wrote: 'All my love, sacred and profane. G.'

Gavin was a loving and thoughtful father and there are echoes of his father's letters to him during the previous war. Gavin sent many postcards to Jenifer and Jeremy between 1939 and 1945. One can imagine how important it was for the children, whose father was away for months at a time, to receive these postcards depicting exotic and far-flung locations. While picture cards only provided enough space for him to write a few lines, he clearly chose them carefully, hoping the photo or painting on the card would be interesting or amusing to them.

In a 1942 postcard to Jenifer, then 13, he wrote, 'your letters have become intensely interesting and informative. What a conscientious girl you are.' On another, he wrote, 'two more cards for your gallery. This one appeals to me greatly. Please write now and then. Dad.'

Around this time, on a card to Jeremy, he wrote: 'Dear Jerem. Don't worry about cricket. I had to play it for years and never liked it, never could play decently. It's a pity – my fault – we didn't get a bat and have some backyard practice last holidays.' Another card displayed a photo of Parliament House, Canberra. 'How goes school? This icing cake picture will make you restless and keen to be here basking in the sun. I am still in Canberra stuck. It is most irritating, but the people I must see are not available.'

In the meantime, Gavin Long's plan for the history evolved to recognise three distinct readerships: first and foremost, the interested general public; second, the participants in the actual events, including service and support personnel, decision-makers and advisers; and third, future historians.

He believed there was widespread community interest in learning the truth about the war. He wanted to follow Bean's insistence to make generous use of photographs and maps, despite criticism at the time that such things belonged to journalism, not history. He paid attention to trends in English historical writing at the time. The *Times Literary Supplement* had declared in 1949 that the historian must write so that he (in 1949, it was invariably a 'he') could be read by a large public. So-called 'good writing' had become as essential for the modern historian as getting the facts right.

For Long the journalist, good writing for a wide readership was as much about style as substance. When crafting his own narratives of a people at war, he revealed that he had in his mind the intimate and grim detail of Tolstoy's *Sevastopol Sketches*. The influence can be seen in the following example of Tolstoy describing Sevastopol in December 1854:

> The flush of morning has but just begun to tinge the sky above Sapun Mountain … the morning frost pinches the face and crackles underfoot … and the thunder of firing in Sevastopol … disturbs the calm of the morning … you listen to the monotonous sound of voices which fly to you over the water, and the grand sounds of firing … increasing in Sevastopol. It cannot be that, at the thought that you too are in Sevastopol, a certain feeling of manliness, of pride has not penetrated your soul, and that the blood has not begun to flow more swiftly through your veins.[13]

Long described the opening of the Battle of Bardia on 3 January 1941 with similar prose:

> At 2.30 am, the men ate a meal and drank their rum and at 4.16 the leading companies began to move forward to the start line in silence except for the swish of feet in the dry soil and low camel-brush … It was pitch dark … the barrage opened with a sudden sustained hammering of guns which lit up the horizon with a line of flashes and streaks of light. The sudden noise, the flash of guns, the sound of shells going overhead and crashing in the darkness had an exhilarating effect … The men began calling, singing and shouting defiance at the enemy, the guns drowning their voices.[14]

The second readership Long wanted to reach comprised the participants themselves. Curtin had told Long he was convinced that an official history was needed because the servicemen would demand it. Long agreed. This readership, too, influenced the approach to style as well as substance. Long believed that 'the chronicler who is dealing with such richly human source material as ours, practically all of it hitherto unexplored and much of it perhaps to remain untouched by other hands for many years, is likely to wish to stand between the reader and the actors no more than necessary'.[15] When crafting their prose, Bean and Long both preferred the 'purple' passages to come directly from the participants rather than from the authors. This applied to the private servicemen, not just the commanding officers. Privates or corporals on patrol and young pilot officers who had made an escape through enemy territory were capable of producing compelling narratives.

The following two examples illustrate Long's point. In chapter 14 of his second volume, *Greece, Crete and Syria*, Long provides a vivid, sometimes thrilling and detailed chronicle of the forced evacuation of Allied troops from Crete in June 1941. The chapter is typically peppered with first-hand reports, diary entries and memoirs of participants. Long includes a lengthy verbatim excerpt from the personal account of a West Australian private, Stanley Carroll, who set out from Crete in a fishing boat with a length of driftwood as a mast and a sail made from some ancient canvas he found in a flour mill. He had intended to sail along the coast looking for companions but was fired upon several times by German aircraft each time he headed into shore, so he elected to attempt to sail to Egypt over 500 kilometres away. He had with him six tins of chocolate and two gallons of water. On the morning of his eighth day at sea, with land in sight, the exhausted and half-blinded Carroll was sailing with one hand and bailing with the other. Long elected to print over 500 words verbatim from Carroll's vividly detailed account. This excerpt illustrates why:

> Hoping the planks would hold out long enough, I kept on and sighted land about 0800 hours. I gave her every bit of canvas she had, not caring a hang what happened now. About 1000 hours she began to leak badly, forward on the port side. With still a good distance to go the water commenced to beat me; trying to bail and steer at the same time was impossible, I couldn't keep my

> feet. Land appeared to be only a few miles off but it must have been nearer ten.
>
> When the boat filled and overturned and the mast smashed a hole in the bottom, my dreams of sailing into Alexandria went with it. Tying my tunic to the rudder clamps I fixed the water tin, almost empty now, across my shoulders and struck out for the shore. It took me seven hours to reach land, swimming, floating and surfing. From the crest of the waves I could see the breakers pounding on the rocks and dashing spray feet into the air. Fortunately I was able to work my way along to a small patch of sand and came ashore, the breakers spinning me around in all directions. I had to crawl on my hands and knees, feeling too giddy to walk.
>
> I drank most of the water I had left, wrung the water out of my trousers, the only article of clothing I had, and started inland. After walking for about an hour I came across an air force listening post. A message was sent to control and next morning I was taken to Mersa Matruh.[16]

The second example, written by South Australian Staff Sergeant F Turner, was appended to the war diary of the 2/43th Battalion after the Australian advance on Beaufort in Borneo. It paints a vivid picture of the actions of Private Starcevich, who was awarded the Victoria Cross for his actions in silencing a Japanese machine gun post. Almost 200 words of Turner's account were reproduced verbatim in chapter 20 of Long's *The Final Campaigns*:

> Fired upon at once by a second LMG, Starcevich, standing in full view of the gunners, cooly charged his magazine and then advanced upon this second post. Starcevich is possessed of a method of approach which in itself must be most disconcerting to an enemy. Firmly and confidently believing that he can never be hit, he walks into an enemy post preceded by a single and

> unbroken stream of pellets. He is quite unmoved by returning fire and stops only when the enemy has been annihilated.

A feature of Long's official history, as with Bean's, was the diligent gathering of biographical information about every participant named in a narrative. These were footnoted on almost every page 'thus to an extent defining the human nature of the force and authenticating the story'.[17] Long devised a proforma to be duplicated and circulated by the staff to participants or their relatives to accurately gather the information and provide a uniform biographical sketch. Footnotes provide name and final rank, honours, service number, affiliation in this instance and the future, as well as birth date and place and occupation. For example, on the first page of his chapter on the Battle of Bardia in his volume *To Benghazi*, Long describes the work of an intelligence officer, Lieutenant Ferguson, in laying 5000 yards of signal wire to mark the route to a crucial landmark. The following footnote is attached:

> Lt-Col I.B. Ferguson, DSO, MC, NX2654; 2/2 Bn. CO 3 Bn RAR, Korea, 1950-51. Journalist; of Potts Point, NSW; b. Wellington, NZ, 13 Apr 1917.

If a participant in the narrative is deceased at the time of writing, that too was noted. In chapter 3 of George Odgers' volume *Air War Against Japan, 1943–1945*, RAAF Flying Officer Austin is described piloting a Hudson bomber in an air attack in April 1943. His footnote reads:

> F-Lt J.S. Austin, DFC, 400363. 608 Sqn RAF; 32, 13 and 2 Sqns. Stock agent; of Lara, Vic; b. Melbourne, 15 May 1918. Died on active service 9 Nov 1943.

For Gavin Long, there was a third and final group of readers – future historians, researchers, educators and academics. Bean said that the completed history 'had to be written so as to carry its proof on its face'. To achieve this 'proof' as reliably as possible, Long and his writers oversaw the drafting, checking and redrafting of chapters with as many vested interests as practically possible. In the preface to his first volume, he wrote:

> While writers and editor have on occasion only reached agreement after considerable discussion, in no case was agreement impossible. Each writer has been given opportunities to read and comment on the drafts of those other writers whose work runs parallel with his own, and, making the most of one of the advantages enjoyed by a contemporary historian, has had his whole work or parts of it read by men who participated in the events he describes.[18]

Long was in a transport aircraft somewhere between Morotai and Balikpapan on 15 August 1945 when he heard the news of the Japanese surrender. He knew then that his work as official historian was about to enter a new phase. By the time the revised plan was approved towards the end of 1945, Long was projecting a series of 17 volumes, plus a one-volume short history to be completed by 1954. He hoped the team could produce three to four volumes per year between 1947 and 1954. He said to Bean at that time that he was hoping to spend as much as three-quarters of his time on his own volumes, but he wondered if there might develop something of a 'tussle' between the claims of the work as a whole and his own sections of it.

In fact, he could not have foreseen the great 'tussle' that would develop in the years ahead. At that time, he had only confirmed six of the writers who would produce the eventual 22 volumes (see chapter 10 for a full description of the writers), and the obstacles encountered by the team would be relentless. He wrote, 'When the war ended I pictured us soon steaming ahead at a great rate. Three months of peace has shown that there is to be no great increase in our rate or progress for some time.'[19]

A potential calamity confronted the project in January 1948 when Gavin was quietly hospitalised in Sydney to have a lymphosarcoma removed from around his right iliac artery. The surgery, followed by three weeks of radiation therapy, was successful. Very few people were privy to the reasons for the hospitalisation at the time. Decades later, he described the cancer scare confidentially to Bill Sweeting as a 'painless malady'. Sweeting shrewdly concluded that the threat of the cancer's return probably hung over his friend for the rest of his working life, driving him as 'a man with no time to spare'. As it turned out, by the time Long formally retired from the project in 1963, after giving it 20 years of his life, it was not yet complete. The final volume in the 22-volume series – Butlin's *War Economy: 1942–1945* – was not published until 1977, almost 10 years after the cancer returned and Gavin Long died.

# 8

# ASSEMBLING THE NARRATIVES

*It was the largest historical project ever undertaken in Australia.*

Bill Sweeting[1]

As general editor and one of the writers of the official history, it was incumbent upon Gavin Long to establish procedures that would bring the project to fruition and deliver the results to as wide a readership as possible. He continually developed and refined these procedures. Throughout the late 1940s and early 1950s, he articulated his approach to his team of writers, in periodic circulars and in various conference papers he was invited to deliver.

Long knew that he must be clear-minded about the immediate aim of his work. He concluded that the aim was not to contribute to a philosophy of war, where 'one short volume should suffice to cover every relevant aspect of Australian experience'; neither was it to educate staff officers, where the historian 'should record orders in detail and write at length about logistics, but only sparingly about what happened at the front line'.[2] Rather, the aim was to chronicle the experiences of a nation at war. In this case, 'the emphasis should be the definition of precisely what happened to the men behind the guns and to the society they represented; to answer why, when it came to the point where decisions were in the hands of small groups of armed men, did they succeed or fail?' Crucially, the history should illuminate whether campaign participants 'were weary or fresh, hungry or fed, high-spirited or downcast, expert or inexpert, well-led or ill. And if the chronicle is to convince, mere general assertions on these points will not be enough.'

In 1961, in his preface to *The Final Campaigns*, he articulated this further, reinforcing his view that the historian primarily is a chronicler, responsible to the truth as far as it can be known, not a polemicist or 'magistrate'. He expanded on this, explaining that, in general, the writers of each volume 'have been hesitant to pass judgment', preferring to describe the events and their outcome and then to 'set out the opinions of those who bore the responsibility or part of it'.[3] The inclinations and opinions of the writer are, however, evident indirectly in his 'selection and presentation of evidence and contemporary opinion'.

A survey of the prefaces to each of the volumes in the official history series suggests five broad objectives envisaged by Long and shared by the writers. The example and influence of Bean are clearly discernible in these objectives, but Long developed them and articulated them more clearly than Bean. The primary objective was to write in such a way that the interested general public would find the work intelligible, informative and satisfying. Long revealed that, in the preparation of his volumes, he was indebted to his wife, 'to whom this volume was read in order that verbal infelicities and obscure terminology might be detected'. John Herington, author of the Air Force volumes *Air War Against Germany and Italy 1939–1943* and *Air Power Over Europe 1944–1945*, explained that he 'aimed to please not the military expert but the citizen'.[4] David Mellor wanted his volume *The Role of Science and Industry* to be 'intelligible to the layman ... with enough detail to make it interesting as well'.[5]

A second objective was to engage the reader in the experiences of the men and women whose exploits were being described. For example, Barton Maugham, in his volume in the Army series *Tobruk and El Alamein*, aimed 'to relate not only what governments arranged and generals ordered and what results they achieved, but also how these were accomplished by the soldiers themselves. Their trials, their triumphs, their disasters.'[6]

A third objective was to relate things that happened in chronological order and primarily from the vantage point of the players in the drama. Douglas Gillison, in his air power volume *Royal Australian Air Force, 1939–1942*, described his aim 'to resist the temptation to introduce evidence provided by "hindsight" and not available to those making the decisions at the time'.[7] This was also a key feature of Bean's history.

The objective was to provide a compelling story, providing a realistic description of events as they unfolded.

A fourth broad objective was to be as fair as possible to the subjects of the narratives. Paul Hasluck, in his volumes *The Government and the People, 1939–1941* and *The Government and the People, 1942–1945*, applied 'an element of discretion and a desire to be fair' to those named in the events described.[8] This attention to fairness was expressed by Long in advice to writers about the use of unit histories: 'The three dangers to be guarded against in unit histories: 1) unjust criticism of the unit on the flank; 2) unjust criticism of the commander; 3) unjust criticism of Allies.'[9] At the outset, Long recognised that criticism, expressed or implied, may be inevitable from time to time, but insisted that 'it should be supported by convincing evidence'.[10]

Finally, the aim was also to focus on the *Australian* story without neglecting the global context. Hasluck developed his narrative in this regard with 'a conscious narrowness'. Lionel Wigmore, in his volume in the Army series of the official history, *The Japanese Thrust*, went one step further, explaining that consideration of the global context required the writer to 'overstep the boundaries of an exclusively national viewpoint', by incorporating examples of those times Australia's participation had an 'influence upon the decisions of her Allies and the reasons which underlay her own decisions'.[11]

To achieve these objectives, the team addressed three questions when planning the projected volumes. Firstly, how to best gather and manage the raw materials – verifiable accounts of events, official documents, photographs – all of which needed to be indexed, copied, stored and extracted. Secondly, how to best guide a team of writers and researchers to assemble narratives in a unified, accurate and interesting way. Finally, how to best design and produce the volumes ready for printing – determining chapter and volume lengths, collecting and drawing maps, curating photographs, and generating chapter footnotes and volume indexes.

Impinging on these three questions were the administrative and bureaucratic realities to be negotiated and managed – liaison with domestic and foreign military and civilian agencies, and management of budgets and facilities, staff, logistics and equipment. Long took upon himself the bulk of the responsibility for overseeing this complex, evolving mosaic, while still writing his own volumes. It is not surprising that the task consumed 20 years of his life.

He discovered early on that these administrative challenges would rarely be solved simply or quickly. For example, throughout August and September 1943, one of the pressing issues to be addressed was division of responsibilities. Treloar bowed out of any involvement almost immediately, except for budgeting for publication. Arthur Bazley was given the responsibility of handling correspondence regarding departmental histories and filling in for Long when he was away. The AWM Board was asked to clarify the delineation of duties between director, assistant director and general editor, as well as to make plans for staff and office space for the history project for years to come. Treloar was not inclined to assist with any of this, expecting that the historians' small staff would do all that Bean's staff had done.

The administrative challenges continued unabated for years. A diary entry towards the end of 1950, seven years into the project, reveals something of Long's weariness. 'There has never been such a pile of work in front of me', he wrote, 'and it will be difficult to have my first volume revised finally by January 31. However, the holiday time will help.'[12]

In a letter to the Secretary of the Department of the Interior five years later, arguing for an increase in editors' and staff salaries, he laid out the demands of the tasks he faced.[13] He wryly described this letter to his son, Jeremy, as 'my impolite memo' that was 'not intended as a model of how to make friends and influence people'. In it, under seven headings, he attempted to describe the complexity and size of the task. He began by reminding the Public Service Board of Commissioners that 'ours is the largest historical project ever undertaken in Australia' and that, unlike official history projects in other countries, he, as the general editor, was also doing a large part of the writing. He further pointed out that the publishing responsibilities in other countries were 'taken over by a fully-equipped university or government publisher', whereas his office was undertaking almost all of the publishing work. In addition, of all the other national projects, except for that of New Zealand, 'ours is the only official war history in which one editor is responsible for histories not only of all three services but of wartime governmental and economic developments' and that these relatively larger burdens were being carried by smaller staffs than in other countries. Both pride and frustration can be discerned in Long's forthright entreaties.

When it came to how best to gather and manage the raw materials for the writers, Long followed Bean's approach, albeit on a far larger and more diverse scale. In May 1943, in addition to the diaries Long maintained, he began to develop the first of 120 handwritten notebooks. But upon examining the records held by the MHS in Melbourne, it became evident to him almost immediately that there were significant gaps, particularly in the early campaigns, that would need to be filled before writers could even attempt their volumes. The notebooks contain interviews with hundreds of officers and men who were able to fill many of these gaps. Long's friend and compatriot, Bill Sweeting, observed that 'without them [the notebooks], it is doubtful whether adequate histories of the campaigns in Libya, Greece, Crete, Syria or in the islands north of Australia, beginning with Papua in 1942 could have been written'. Sweeting accompanied Long on some of these fact-finding expeditions and recalled that he often marvelled at Long's method of note-taking, observing that he recorded his interviews 'in a kind of abbreviated longhand', frequently only recording the first letter or the first syllable of a word, 'methodically spacing each in such a way that he or I was able easily to fill out the words at a later stage'.[14] It was then Sweeting's job to oversee the indexing of the notebooks.

Stewart Jamieson, RAAF Intelligence Officer, diplomat and later Australian High Commissioner, reflected on the interviewing style that led to the detailed notes Gavin Long was able to gather from soldiers of all ranks. Jamieson likened Long to US newspaperman Scotty Reston, who, according to a US Secretary of State, was successful because 'he does the work and troubles to ask the right questions'. Long, he went on, 'worked immensely hard to know the subject thoroughly before he started to question the authorities in any field in which he was writing. As a result, he got from the expert the eager response of one who recognises knowledge and insight.'[15]

From the outset, securing reliable source materials was a critical challenge. As Long put it, 'In the early years, the problem remained of discovering what was where'.[16] Vast quantities of Army records remained unsorted, and yet the records of the Department of Defence, including those of the War Cabinet, 'were comprehensive and in apple-pie order'.

A complicating factor in the already fraught process of gathering and curating records was the fact that the responsibility for collecting Army records was spread between the AWM in Canberra and the MHS in Melbourne. Treloar, who was both AWM director and, until 1946, the officer-in-charge of the MHS, believed his priority was to gather the materials before they were lost. In his mind, sorting and curating could be done later, once materials were safely collected. Long's priority, however, was to access these growing mountains of unarchived material.

The gathering of materials after the end of the war was further complicated by all the administrative realities of the demobilisation process. Some records were lost or destroyed before they could be secured. Long noted an example of his anxiety in a diary entry in October 1945.[17] He had become aware of a very large cache of files belonging to the British Ministry of Information in Delhi relating to the fall of Singapore. These files contained 'very frank criticisms of policy and of important people, some of it by men who were still in the public service'. Realising the great value of these documents and their sensitivity, and that 'if the files were asked for on a high level there would be great delay and probably the British government would not be willing to hand them over', he instructed researcher John Galvin to go through the files and make copies of any papers he thought might be valuable. He was then to hand these over to the Australian High Commissioner to India, General Mackay. This required Galvin's small staff to commit to immense amounts of typing as there was only one typist in the High Commissioner's office in Delhi!

The process was further complicated by the fact that small teams with limited resources were attempting to gather records that had been generated before the war's end in widely scattered, multinational, multi-service operations. These records had often been censored. In September 1943, Hermon Gill confirmed to Long that he was willing to be the naval historian for the series and that a naval historical section was now operating, overseen by himself. He and his lone assistant would begin collecting documents while at sea, during trips to Britain, the United States and the Middle East. It would not be until July 1946 that Gill and the naval historical records section would boast a staff of 12, including four researchers. As for Air Force records, there was no Air Force historical section, nor even a proposal to establish one until as late as September 1944. It was approved towards the end of that month with a staff of 15.

Gavin Long defined three 'levels' of source material. First, there were upper-level materials, including government minutes, reports and correspondence. While most of this material was formally recorded and stored, there was a need to seek out informal records arising from conversations. In July 1945, he expressed his concern to Fred McLaughlin, formerly private secretary to Prime Minister Curtin, that it might now be difficult to collect an adequate account of Curtin's conversations with General MacArthur, and other informal negotiations in which Curtin had had a leading role.[18]

Long stressed that the project needed as much information as possible from those conversations between Curtin and MacArthur, but encountered resistance from McLaughlin, who believed that prime ministerial conversations ought to remain secret. Long reminded him that, even in the years immediately following the end of the 1914–18 war, even though secrecy was held sacrosanct by many in high office, 'within a few years, men such as Lloyd George and Churchill had published very frank and full memoirs of the war'. He pressed upon McLaughlin the urgency of obtaining written records of important negotiations before it was too late, assuring him that such records could, for the time being, be securely stored. McLaughlin reluctantly assured Long that he would 'see someone whom he had in mind'. Long concluded that he meant Shedden, who, as Secretary of the Department of Defence since 1937, principal adviser to prime ministers Menzies, Curtin and Chifley, and Secretary of the Advisory War Council during the war, had played a significant role in War Cabinet discussions and was arguably the person most intimately familiar with the 'secrets' that so concerned McLaughlin.

For Long, the second level of materials comprised Cabinet documents and senior commanders' reports, and the third level was war diaries and other operational records. This third level was most commonly used by military historians.

War diaries, the day-to-day records of events maintained by each Army unit, were submitted monthly to the Central Army Records Office, but Long soon discovered gaps in these records. In 1943, he read some brigade and battalion diaries from the New Guinea and Greek campaigns held at the MHS.[19] He immediately discovered that the quality of the diaries, from the historian's perspective, ranged from 'good to very defective'. He noted that 'diaries seldom contain references to names of junior officers or descriptions of living conditions, tactics and incidents'. He saw that supplementary materials would be necessary. He was struck that the written accounts of the three battles in Greece were so brief that 'I think the solution here is to ask all infantry, artillery and engineer units to append narratives written by all surviving company and platoon commanders'.

Long was pleased to note that the quality of the records in the diaries did tend to improve as the war went on, partly because of training and better facilities, but also, as Long put it, 'because as the war grew older, the soldiers saw themselves more clearly as playing a part in events which would be recorded in their nation's history'.[20]

Long himself provided informal training to officers to help them improve the quality of their unit diaries. While visiting the 4th Armoured Brigade at Southport in Queensland in June 1944, he advised commissioned and non-commissioned officers about the things they should keep in mind when compiling their war diaries, remembering that the object of the diary was to teach lessons about the campaign that could provide material for both unit and national histories. He recommended that their diaries include lists of officers and their exact postings, appended reports and documents, and that they ought always to err on the side of appending too much. They should use names rather than just titles or roles, append citations for gallantry and include a medical officer's after-action report. Then, while in camp, they should write periodical reviews of discipline, amenities and conditions, and describe the life of the unit generally.

Long discussed the topic of Australian Army war diaries in a 1957 address he gave to the Canberra Historical Society, which was published in *Stand-To* journal in 1963.[21] Modelled on British diaries, he explained, they typically opened with a day-to-day account of the month's events entered on a printed form. However, a conscientious officer in a busy month might add many pages to these forms comprising copies of signals, company and patrol reports, statistics, letters, orders and medical reports for that month. Long found that the medical officers' reports were often of great value to the historian. He gave the example of an infantry battalion diary chronicling the battalion's approach to the Aitape–Wewak campaign in 1945. The diary recorded bare facts about how the unit had pressed on and carried out each assigned task, but the medical officer's report provided further insights: 'Exhaustion, nervous strain and malaria now uncontrollable. C.O. informed that the battalion could no longer carry on.'

The quality of the war diaries depended on the individuals who kept them. Some war diaries answered almost every conceivable question for the historian – names, maps, sketches, 'lively and detailed narrative and uninhibited comment' – while others were not only sketchy but ambiguous. Conditions also played a part in the quality and quantity of the content of the diaries. As an example, Long cited an important unit diary he had read that had been written in pencil 'in a six-penny exercise book' in the Owen Stanley ranges in 1942 because it had not been possible to carry typewriters, duplicating machines or tracing paper.

Long knew that, in addition to Australian war diaries, the project was going to need records from the Americans in the Southwest Pacific theatre and from Britain for North Africa, the Mediterranean and Malaya. With MacArthur's blessing, he and Bill Sweeting lived and worked with the Americans, initially in the historical division at headquarters in the T & G Building in central Brisbane and later with the US 6th Division in Hollandia and the 41st US Division in Biak.

Alongside the war diaries were the recorded recollections of individuals. These recollections often provided vivid glimpses into events and people and were greatly coveted by Long and the other writers, especially if they had been recorded on the day in question, or very soon after. Long was fond of the observation of British General Sir Ian Hamilton, who said of Gallipoli that 'on the actual day of battle, naked truths may be picked up for the asking; by the following morning they have already begun to get into their uniforms'.[22] Indeed, Hamilton would spend decades grooming and smoothing his own 'uniform' following his many grievous errors during the Gallipoli campaign.

Long and Sweeting discovered that it was still fruitful to interview first-hand participants, even if some time had passed. In their experience of Australians at war, memories did not fade quite so quickly as one might expect and it was often advantageous to interview troops who were rested rather than weary. 'I have sat with some company commanders for up to three hours', he later recalled, 'while they talked on and on, describing in precise detail a long action that took place some time before'. But it had to be first-hand recollections if possible. Second-hand or third-hand evidence was suspect. Long went further than Hamilton by quipping that, by the time a story has been repeated by someone who heard it from someone else, 'it has probably begun to get, not into uniform, but into fancy dress'.[23]

In 1944, Gavin Long advised Flight Lieutenant Les Jillett, head of the newly formed RAAF historical records section, to instruct his staff how to interview Air Force personnel in Australia, India, the Middle East and Britain. They were to approach the task as if they were novelists of the future, seeking to write a rousing tale about the RAAF of the present. This approach should include discovering 'what the troops wear, eat, how they live, how they amuse themselves off duty, what they read, their opinions and their grouches, sketches of outstanding leaders, and their slang'.[24]

A further developing source for the writers in the years after the war was the work being undertaken by German historians and many documents secured from captured enemy soldiers. Long enthused, 'we can now write about what was happening on "the other side of the hill" in about as much detail as we can write about our own side'. He cited the example of the personal diaries of captured Japanese soldiers that were sometimes so detailed as to enable a reconstruction of Japanese plans and operations in fairly close detail, despite the Japanese authorities having destroyed many documents at the end of the war. 'It would be grim', he observed, 'if the historian had to rely solely on post-war Japanese interrogations'.[25]

As the gathering and archiving of information continued apace, Long sought to ensure that his writers drafted their narratives with a fairly strict adherence to chronological sequence. As the writers drafted the content of their chapters, they broadly followed a twofold process – painstakingly drawing together and blending multiple source materials into a coherent narrative, and then seeking to critique and improve its quality and veracity. Lionel Wigmore described it as a process of combining sources from those closest to the action 'for experience' with official records 'for context'.[26] In the preface to his volume, he pointed to interviews and correspondence with leading civil and military authorities; formation, unit and sub-unit commanders; and men whose principal jobs were to use their weapons, drive a truck, maintain a telephone line and so on. All these, by relating what they did, saw or experienced at particular times and places, helped to confirm, correct or amplify information contained in the records.

Long's policy was to always prefer the evidence of a witness close to the event in place and time to one farther away. For example, a company commander's report was preferred to a brigade's account of the same incident. Long knew that the narratives he and his writers drew together would sooner or later be open to critical examination by 'those who were on the spot'.

In the prefaces to their respective volumes, some of the authors also described the difficulties they had encountered when assembling their narratives. These ranged from a paucity of source materials to an overabundance, requiring considerable assistance to sort through. John Herington was faced with a paucity of materials when assembling his narratives about the air war in Europe and the Middle East. As he explained, his challenge arose from Australian airmen having been spread among more than 500 squadrons of the RAF, more than half of which were not required to provide operational records to Australian authorities. He was unable to fill gaps in the record by interviewing participants because 'a very high proportion of them were dead'.

Then there were the seemingly less significant yet frequent difficulties relating to place names. Many were transcribed from other languages – Greek, Arabic, Indonesian – and some were not even in existence until they were coined by participants in actions there. Long was aware of this difficulty from the beginning. In late 1943, while in Port Moresby, he encouraged intelligence staff to keep a record of the origin of place names in New Guinea, especially the names of places where battles were fought, 'names … which have been given to otherwise nameless places by the army'.[27]

When he began the official history, Long had never drafted a narrative about a campaign in which he had not personally witnessed events and interviewed participants, yet he knew that assembling a narrative 'from a distance' could be trusted to yield a result that was reliably factual as well as interesting. It was his aim to choose writers who were not personally involved in the events they would be writing about so they would not be open to accusations of personal bias.

To test the process, in September 1943, he began drafting a narrative of the Australian 7th Division's Lebanon campaign. He had never been to Lebanon, so he was not personally familiar with the country or the events being described. Curiously, he incorrectly referred to it repeatedly as 'Syria'. Despite this, after gathering the information from battalion and brigade commanders who had been there and who, importantly, had agreed to read and re-read his manuscript, he discovered that an acceptable narrative was indeed possible for one who had never visited a particular location, provided the writer had access to detailed company narratives and adequate maps. He was careful to take detailed notes of any points of criticism made by his advisers, all the while maintaining, as far as possible, the critical perspective of the historian. He did not merely accept criticisms at face value, even from the most senior of commanders, if he felt that the criticisms did not accord with the evidence. For example, when General Rowell, who, under General Blamey, had helped prepare and lead the 6th Division in the Middle East, objected to a point in Long's analysis of the Greek campaign, Long discussed the matter with him. Subsequently, he noted in his diary that 'after a longish discussion, Rowell withdrew his criticism'.[28]

Gavin Long proved to be an effective and widely respected team leader, marshalling his troops to work productively and generally harmoniously with meagre resources and inadequate facilities. The teamwork itself was a vital element of the entire project, and its well-managed success stands as a testament to its leader.

# 9
# HIS DEVOTED STAFF

*I know how greatly I am indebted to him. By precept and example, he was in every way an inspiration to those who worked with him, not only the writers of the history volumes, but his devoted staff at Canberra.*

G Hermon Gill[1]

Throughout 1945, Gavin Long fretted about how long it was taking to gather a staff of researchers, sometimes called 'narrators', at other times 'literary assistants'. He worried that his writers would be overwhelmed as soon as the war ended, anticipating that 'truckloads of stationery and unit papers would be arriving and they would need all the staff they could muster. After the last war, hundreds of troops awaiting demobilisation were employed for months on this work.'[2]

As writers were being slowly recruited, the priority in Long's mind at that time was staff. He was quite sure that it would not unduly disadvantage the project if writers were unable to begin their work full-time for a year or so. It was to be expected that some of the wartime secretiveness in the departments would take a little while to dissipate, and the histories would be a little further along by then. The urgency focused on staff work – the gathering and managing of documents.

John Treloar, though initially supportive, had his own challenges after returning to the AWM. He clearly did not see the official history as his priority. In 1944, he surprised Long by indicating through Arthur Bazley that he preferred to have very little to do with the project. 'I think', he wrote to Bazley, 'that I should have nothing to do with the plans for the history except in so far as the arrangements for publication and distribution affect the War Memorial Fund'. He further directed that the responsibility for guiding the historical sections, the departmental histories and unit histories, would be Long's and, at Long's delegation, Bazley's.

Long had assumed that Treloar would be anxious to approve all matters relating to the history as he was the 'eventual custodian of all service records' and had already advised the Navy and Air Force officers concerned that this would be the case. It wasn't that Treloar was giving Long his blessing and assuring him of minimal interference, it was that he saw the project as one more bothersome set of difficulties for which he had little enthusiasm. Long's requests from Treloar were repeatedly met with a cool reception at best and resistance at worst. He even resisted Long's approach to have Bill Sweeting appointed, objecting that there were already too many sergeants on staff. Long seems to have had a much warmer and more productive relationship with Bazley, but he could not avoid dealing with the curmudgeonly Treloar.

There were additional misunderstandings and complications for Long in his dealings with the government. When Senator Collings introduced him to the new Minister for the Interior, Herbert Johnson, in July 1945, Long discovered that Johnson knew nothing about the history plan, nor even that it came under his department. Long had to begin from scratch with him. Often there were difficulties securing approvals from the Public Service Board. Commissioner Frank Thorpe refused to designate a woman 'senior research assistant' because no women in the service were paid at that level. He required she be designated 'research assistant' on a lower salary band. Thorpe also complained that the term 'research officer' was being too freely used and suggested 'literary assistant' for staff. By 1950, Long was legitimately worried that staff would leave the team, lured away by offers of higher salaries. Of the four literary assistants at that time, three were looking elsewhere or had found other jobs, and the fourth was likely to follow. Fearing the loss of experience and knowledge this would entail, he raised his concerns with the Public Service Board but was met with more sympathy than action.

The first team member to be appointed was Nancy Penman, a Sydney University graduate who had worked in the New South Wales Premier's Department. Penman was hard-working, competent and versatile, with a gentle sense of humour to match Long's. She was based at the AWM, but during the war, her duties included travelling throughout Queensland wherever Australian and American troops were stationed, gathering records that would eventually inform Paul Hasluck's volumes. Bill Sweeting recalled that on such excursions, Nancy had a knack for observation – picking up impressions from local civic leaders and police about the impact on their communities of large numbers of bivouacked troops.

Long, Bazley and Penman began experimenting in September 1944 with a card file index system for keeping track of personal narratives, biographical information and diaries. To get things underway, Long placed an initial order with the government printing office for 10 000 index cards and 200 cloth-bound notebooks. He had in mind a system that could readily be expanded to enable the staff to keep up with the influx of materials he expected after the war ended.

Sergeant Bill Sweeting was the second appointee to the official history staff. He was a veteran of 7th Division campaigns in the Middle East and New Guinea and was seconded to the Department of the Interior in June 1944. He joined the official history team as senior research officer, a role he would discharge with efficiency and flair until Long's retirement in 1963, at which point he took charge of the staff. Sweeting and Long became fast friends and, of Long's many colleagues, he probably knew him best. His essay, 'Gavin Long, war historian: A memoir', published in the *Canberra Historical Journal* in 2007, has, until now, been the most comprehensive and intimate memoir of Long's life. Sweeting's contribution cannot be overstated. He and Gavin frequently travelled together on field expeditions. He oversaw the completion of the bulk of the research about Australian prisoners of the Japanese, which he contributed in three chapters to Lionel Wigmore's volume *The Japanese Thrust*. He also drafted 'Ordeal on New Britain', which appears as Appendix 4 in that volume.

In 1946, Mary Gilchrist joined the staff as a literary assistant and, in Long's words, 'steered the organisation through its administrative problems'. She remained with the project until its completion and prepared volumes for the printers, including the exacting task of compiling indexes. In the preface to *The Six Years War*, Long wrote: 'Mary Gilchrist, who detected some errors and inconsistencies in the drafts, chose the illustrations and wrote the index. This volume and the history as a whole owe much to her continued devotion to the task.'[3]

Later that same year, Captain John Balfour, who had been seconded to the MHS and had been designated Australia's historical representative to MacArthur's headquarters, joined the team as a senior research officer alongside Sweeting. Balfour had a long acquaintance with Bean's official history, having travelled with Bean's mission to Gallipoli in 1919 and worked on his staff until that history's completion in 1942.

It was also in 1946 that John Treloar decided the official history staff should relocate – the first of six such moves, each one considerably disrupting the team's operations – to more expansive premises in the old Canberra Hospital building at Acton. Secret documents were to be housed in the disused mortuary. Sweeting recalled that official war artist, Bill Dargie, willingly assisted with the move, there being no other males about to help, 'Gavin having disappeared into the smoke as he always did when a shift of quarters was involved'.

By the beginning of 1947, as Long worked on extract-making and writing, in addition to overseeing administration, the staff settled into working on biographical cards and chronologies, duplicating and organising collections of papers and general research. Hugh Groser began drawing maps of Bardia and Tobruk. Groser, a cartographer and artist who had served as a sergeant with the Army's Land Headquarters cartographic company during the war, was responsible for the hand-drawn maps that are scattered liberally through many of the official history volumes. His superb maps were patiently and laboriously produced, eventually with the help of an assistant cartographer, Elaine Oates. Groser was barely able to keep up with the production of the volumes, some of which contained more than 100 maps specifically relating to the content of that volume alone. In his memoir, Sweeting recalled:

> On more than one occasion, Hugh would be found pen still poised in hand sound asleep at his work. [He was sometimes] more concerned with the beauty of an arrangement than with accuracy, it was often possible to find small errors in practically every map Hugh produced — a transposed letter in a place name, a village or town wrongly placed, an error in the designation of a unit. None of Hugh's mistakes, however, was as mortifying as one detected at a late stage in a map of the Middle East in which 'Red Sea' was designated 'Red Hill'.[4]

As Long conceived it, the principal role of staff was to act as literary assistants. Generally, a small staff of assistants would assemble documents for the authors, check chapters, compile footnotes and indexes, prepare the copy for the printer, sometimes sketch maps for the cartographer, collect and title photographs, and check and re-check the text. Crucially, all of these ancillary tasks were completed by workers who, as Long put it, 'had lived with the volume as long as the author himself'. By designating an assistant to be responsible for a single volume or group of volumes almost from beginning to end, Long ensured continuity and reliability, with assistants becoming specialists in their area of concern. As Sweeting recalled:

> A good literary assistant thus became an author's insurance policy against the ghastly errors to which even the most careful are prone. Gavin Long considered, for example, that better indexes would be done by people with a thorough knowledge of what the volume was about rather than by one who came to it solely as an indexer; that the best illustrations would be selected by someone who knew the volume almost by heart.

At the outset, Long prepared a style guide for writers and staff, and this was amended as the project progressed. The literary assistants would ensure that each writer's typescript complied with the guide. They would also ensure that every location named in the body of the text could be found by the reader on one of the maps in that volume. Some volumes refer to over 1000 place names, many of them only referred to by that name in the context of that volume's story and not appearing on any map beyond it. In addition to being responsible for checking their assigned volumes, literary assistants even took pains to crosscheck with other volumes to avoid contradictions. Sweeting cites the example of the first big Japanese air raids on Darwin in February 1942, which were referenced from various points of view and in varying detail in no fewer than six volumes.

The assistants were also required to conduct research and even contribute to the writing. It was Long's principle that the assistants were never dependent on narratives or summaries prepared by others. This was to ensure that the material was reliable and trustworthy. 'The author's needs were the determining factor', recalls Sweeting. 'If he fell behind, the task of one of the assistants was to help him catch up. In this respect, of course, Gavin Long was a major contributor to all volumes.'

It may be hard to conceive in this age of digital word processing just how much manual work was required to pull together all the elements of 22 volumes of carefully produced content. Indexing, for example, was an essential and immense task. Indexes often contained as many as 15 000 cards, one for each entry in the final volume. Even an experienced indexer might work full-time for three months or more to complete a single volume index. It is worth recalling the technology that the teams had available to them. Manuscripts were handwritten or typed using cumbersome mechanical typewriters, which were capable of generating two or three copies of each page using interleaved sheets of carbon paper. Catalogues of information were stored on index cards kept in drawers or wooden boxes. Documents were duplicated on lumbering Roneo machines or spirit duplicators, or photographed with special Leica cameras to create microfilm, ideal for storage or transport. Photographs were developed by specialists in dark rooms using potent chemicals. Maps were drawn by hand.

Gavin Long was not by nature a technophile, except when it involved the production of film or art, yet the stark realities presented by the sheer size and scope of the official history project demanded that he seek out as many time-saving, cost-effective technological solutions as possible. In July 1945, for example, he investigated the costs of available technologies: microfilming was one penny per page; a microfilm reader was anything up to 20 pounds; a microfilming plant around 300 pounds; enlargements of microfilmed pages were 1 shilling each; photostatting was 1 shilling and sixpence per page; and a typist could be expected to copy a page for 7 pence. The MHS was given approval in 1944, seven months after requesting it, to purchase a Hollerith tabulating machine for compiling statistics and lists. The computer used a system of electrical and mechanical signals, and a set of wires positioned over pools of mercury, to incrementally count data on paper punch cards. That same year, Treloar ordered a microphotography (microfilm) machine. He was keen for GHQ officers to use photography to copy and archive documents.

The assistants were also responsible for the biographical summaries added as footnotes whenever service personnel were named for the first time in a narrative. Some of the information needed for high-profile individuals could be obtained from *Who's Who*. For others, there was the Central Army Records Office in Melbourne. Long devised a printed form for assistants to post to individuals or their relatives asking for additions or corrections. A survey of the footnotes in 'The Battle of Bardia', chapter 8 of *To Benghazi*, reveals 120 entries across 44 pages. Each entry provides name, final rank, service number, units served in, occupation at enlistment, birthplace, date of birth and date of death, if applicable. A small handful of discrepancies is revealed when cross-referenced against the details held by the AWM, National Archives of Australia and government records of Births, Deaths and Marriages. It is intriguing that the footnote for Gavin Long's own brother, Merrick, then a sergeant who received the Military Medal and a recommendation for officer training for his part in that battle, contains an apparent error. Merrick's year of birth is stated there as 1909, but his birth record in Victoria and in the National Archives of Australia reports 1910. By contrast, it is worth noting an example of the attention to accuracy in the explanatory note in the biographical footnote for Ian McIntosh. The National Archives of Australia records, based on McIntosh's enlistment documents, have his birth year as 1905, whereas the footnote in *To Benghazi* has it as 1897. The record is set straight in this way: 'He, like other veterans, had stated on enlistment in 1939, that he was under 35'.

Then there were the illustrations, for which the assistants were also largely responsible. Sweeting explained:

> If a book's quota of illustrations was, say, 80 pictures, the assistant would probably have to search out from collections in service departments, newspaper officers, perhaps half as many again to give the author a choice. The writing of captions was often a problem, largely because of wartime censorship at the time the photographs were taken. We sent copies of pictures to the people we thought would know the answer. It often took a lot of letter-writing before we were sure that we knew precisely what the picture was about.

In 1951, Long prepared to send the completed manuscript of his first volume, *To Benghazi*, to the printers. He reported that, at its maximum, the staff employed to help the writers had included seven research workers or literary assistants, a cartographer, a secretary and two part-time typists. In 1952, the minister approved his request for two additional assistants because of the heavy workload. The Public Service Board only granted one.

Long's responsibility as general editor extended beyond his own team of researchers and assistants. He also sought to offer guidance and provide training for other teams. For example, in April 1948, he met with the fledgling staff and writers at the war history section of the RAAF. He introduced them to the aims and progress of the history, and roles and relationship with the history staff. Writers discussed 'assignments' with their research assistants. In his diary, he noted with impatience that it appeared 'the researchers had the idea that there was no urgent work to do'.[5]

Gavin Long and his team were largely responsible for the final broad challenge after gathering source materials and assembling narratives – that of producing and seeing the final volumes through to publication. He believed that experience with the first history had shown that the AWM would be the best publisher. This, and budget constraints, inevitably meant that almost the entire responsibility for determining the layout and arranging the printing of the volumes of the war history rested upon Long and his staff. Fortunately, in addition to his capacity as a wordsmith, he had a flair for the art and technique of high-quality, hardcover book production. The resulting 22 volumes are an enduring testament to a team that lived up to Bean's ideal of 'capacity and character'.

# 10
# THE GENERATION THAT BELONGS TO THIS WAR

*[This author] owes his greatest debt to the General Editor, Mr Gavin Long. From him he has received unfailing inspiration by precept and example; constant encouragement; sympathetic understanding, and sage editorial comment. His contribution cannot be over-estimated.*

G Hermon Gill[1]

In 1943, Prime Minister Curtin established a War History Committee, comprising the Leader of the Opposition, the Minister for External Affairs and himself (Chifley replaced him after Curtin's death) to consult with Gavin Long and the Minister for the Interior regarding the selection of writers for the series. Only Long, as general editor, and the medical editor were to be salaried. The volume writers were to be contracted for a fee – 2000 pounds for a first volume, less for the next – which would be paid in instalments. They were also required to complete their volumes within a set time, usually four years per volume. It was expected that the writers, most of whom were employed elsewhere, would dedicate a year full-time to their volumes, although several gave considerably longer than that.

Of the 14 men Long proposed to write 19 of the 22 volumes, five were journalists – himself, Lionel Wigmore, George Odgers, Douglas Gillison and Chester Wilmot – and five were academics – John Herington, Paul Hasluck, Sydney Butlin, David Mellor and Boris Schedvin. And while one of them, G Hermon Gill, was a professional naval officer, and more than half of the writers had served in uniform during the war, on Long's insistence, none of them, except David Dexter and Barton Maughan, had been closely involved in directing the affairs about which they would write. This was to ensure that accusations of bias or self-interest were unlikely to be levelled against them. Long's aim was to balance the advantages of an author's first-hand experience of events or places with the disadvantages of having been closely involved as a senior commander. As it turned out, the ranks held by writers who had been commissioned officers ranged from Pilot Officer to Navy Commander and Lieutenant Colonel. Each writer, with the help of the literary assistants, personally researched the primary source materials for their volumes, rather than relying upon materials extracted by others. Another principle Long maintained was that 'each writer should be of the generation that belongs to this war rather than to the last'.[2]

The selection of writers was a fraught and lengthy process for Gavin Long and marked by several tragedies. Long would discuss options with various trusted and expert contacts, only to find that most were unwilling or unavailable, or they'd say, 'not at the present time'. In fact, Long recalled that none of the potential writers he approached 'jumped immediately at the idea, all needing to ask questions and consider ongoing responsibilities'.[3] And committee approvals for those he did recommend were often frustratingly slow in coming. This is not to say the War History Committee was uninterested – opinions were varied and frankly canvassed – but when committee members proposed unsuitable candidates, Long was able to draw on thorough preparation and usually held firm on his recommendations. He had a lengthy discussion with Menzies in April 1944 about the suitability of journalists as writers. Menzies felt that journalists were too slipshod and inaccurate to be reliable historians. Long did not concede this point, but did agree that '9 out of 10 newspapermen did not have the temperament for the work'.[4] As Bill Sweeting put it: 'The overall result was a team of devoted people, most of whom were to find their undertaking far harder than they expected and one which was to remain a millstone around their necks while they battled with their own problems of post-war rehabilitation'.

At their first meeting in March 1943, Long and Bean had considered options for authors, discussing the possibility that Long should write the volume covering the interwar years and the story of the Second AIF up to the end of the operations in Cyrenaica in the first quarter of 1941; Kenneth Slessor be approached for the volume on Greece, Crete and Syria; and Chester Wilmot for the volume about the 9th Division's contribution in North Africa in 1941–42. They agreed to approach anthropologist, academic and North Australia Observer Unit ('Nackeroos') commander William Stanner to write two volumes covering the campaigns against the Japanese in Malaya at the beginning of the war and land operations in the Southwest Pacific up until March 1943. Bean was very impressed with Stanner and also suggested that Long approach him to accept a role as assistant editor of the official history project and as a potential successor to Long 'in case of accident'. It seems Stanner declined both suggestions, but he offered, somewhat whimsically, in December 1945, while impatiently awaiting demobilisation: 'If you think you want urgent advice which only I can give you on the political or economic volume, you may summon me home as soon as you like!'[5] Long did correspond with Stanner, seeking his advice through the 1950s while the research continued on what he styled the 'home front' volumes about the government and the people.

From the outset, Bean's support for Stanner was in stark contrast to his opposition to Slessor. As Long recalled it:

> I suggested that Slessor should write the Greece, Crete, Syria volume. B said that he thought Slessor had not made the most of his opportunities; but that he reckoned the 'tragic and dramatic qualities' of these campaigns might appeal to Slessor. On the other hand, the truth about Syria cannot be discovered without a great amount of work. Would KS find this research irksome and uninteresting? Personally, I would be unhappy if he were not offered the writing of a volume. If he was unwilling, I might have to do it myself.[6]

By June 1943, Long had consulted widely enough to have developed a list that he could begin to reduce 'by process of elimination'. At that time, Bean recommended that unsuitable writers for the civil series would be those whose political leanings might incline them to prove a political point, men who had been leading actors in the administration, or 'men inclined to be inoffensive where criticism was demanded'.[7] In effect, Bean recommended that he find someone who could be counted on to offer criticism where it was warranted, but to do so as objectively and reasonably as possible. For example, in choosing Hasluck, Long had agreed with Menzies about the unsuitability of historian, author and outspoken civil libertarian Brian Fitzpatrick, noting in his diary that he thought Fitzpatrick 'a tendentious writer'. Long told Menzies that he would be reluctant to propose Fitzpatrick, stating that 'in my opinion anything he wrote would be designed to prove a political theory'.[8] Such decisions are subjective, and initial concerns along similar lines might well have been directed at Hasluck, himself a strongly opinionated political player. Hasluck, as it turned out, was a careful, objective historian. Despite Long's reservations, Fitzpatrick was appointed to begin writing the volume. It transpired that Long's concern that he would become tendentious was moot. By mid-1947, Fitzpatrick had a number of other writing projects on the go and was growing increasingly restive. With the task barely begun, he informed Long that he was dropping out. He claimed that he saw 'no usefulness' to his career if he continued with the official history.[9] This was yet another vexing disappointment for Long, but David Mellor was willing to take over from Fitzpatrick and proved a very able writer, producing a fine volume.

The team of writers now comprised Gavin Long, Barton Maughan, Lionel Wigmore, Dudley McCarthy, David Dexter, G Hermon Gill, Douglas Gillison, George Odgers, John Herington, Paul Hasluck, Sydney Butlin, Boris Schedvin, Allan Walker and David Mellor. (Although Walker completed two of his four volumes before illness overtook him, and partially drafted *The Island Campaigns*, necessitating a number of contributors, he is named as author of all four volumes.)

As 1949 began, with the project in its sixth year, Long wrote: 'In this new year, I begin a new routine. Priority will be given to my work as editor and not as writer.'[10] This new routine entailed regular and detailed correspondence with each writer, addressing seemingly never-ending difficulties relating to documents, design, layout and editing of drafts, and slowly compiling notes for the projected one-volume concise history of the war. He attended to the challenges and complexities of managing the team of writers, guiding the staff, seeing to the collecting and archiving of documents, and negotiating with government bodies while facing some serious health issues of his own. As all of this was happening, he managed to complete his first volume, which was first published in 1952.

In February 1949, four years after accepting his task, Allan Walker gave the first indications of the difficult personal issues that would increasingly dog his involvement until his resignation in 1956. Long wrote that Walker was 'very depressed at having no assistant', 'seems to have lost heart' and was 'on the verge of resigning the task'. By June of that year, the weariness is palpable in Long's diary:

> Walker's situation still unresolved. Hasluck says he intends to seek termination of his contract (unclear why this is. Pay dispute?). McCarthy seeking appointment as assistant registrar of ANU, unclear about his future availability. Wigmore still unable to obtain accommodation in Canberra. Gillison in hospital. Herington has done nothing for some time because of 'domestic problems'.[11]

Tragically, some writers were lost. General Rupert Downes, who had enthusiastically begun work on the medical history after Allan Walker initially turned it down, was killed in March 1945 when the Hudson aircraft he was travelling in crashed off the coast of Cairns, killing all on board. Journalist George Fenton, Long's first choice to write the New Guinea volume, subsequently written by Dudley McCarthy, was travelling in an American bomber, which disappeared between Port Moresby and Wau. Chester Wilmot was killed in the crash of a de Havilland Comet in the Mediterranean in 1954. Allan Walker died in 1958, having resigned from his writing commitments due to ill health in 1956.

Barton Maughan's *Tobruk and El Alamein* was first published in 1966. Maughan (1912–1988), a Sydney barrister before the war, served with the 20th Brigade and later transferred to the 9th Division when it sailed to the Middle East. Rejoining it from Mersa Matruh after the failure of Operation Battleaxe, he served as a lieutenant with the 2/13th Battalion throughout most of the subsequent operations described in his volume. He received the Military Cross for 'enterprise, courage and coolness' at Alamein, then served as an intelligence officer and rose to the rank of lieutenant colonel with South East Asia Command in 1945. According to Bill Sweeting, 'Montgomery at an El Alamein reunion in London told Maughan that his account of the battle was the best he had read'.

Maughan was not appointed to write his volume until 1955, replacing Chester Wilmot. Wilmot had been high on Long's list of preferred authors from the beginning, but his appointment was never going to be likely as long as Blamey was alive because of Blamey's animosity towards him. After Blamey's death in 1951, Wilmot was finally appointed, only to die in 1954. Fortuitously, ten years earlier, with the war still raging, Wilmot had willed all of his writings, notebooks and papers to Gavin Long, so Maughan was able to make use of them when he took over.

Chester Wilmot was a talented, charismatic and dedicated journalist and proved himself an excellent historian. His *The Struggle for Europe*, published in 1952, is a superb account of the Allied Normandy invasion. As a war correspondent, he was 'discredited' by Blamey and sent home from New Guinea because he refused to drop a subject Blamey warned him against pursuing. The incident distressed Long, who wrote to Bean in November 1942: 'It is a bad business. Chester has probably seen more action than any English-speaking correspondent in this war. He is keen, learned, and an outstanding radio commentator. This is only one detail in an unhappy picture. It is very distressing to see the army being torn by factions.'[12] Curtin told Long in 1943 that he wanted the list of potential writers to be shown to Blamey for comment and that it would be inadvisable to include Wilmot's name. Wilmot's reporting about Tobruk 'had caused a first class row between Morshead and Lavarack'. Long reassured Curtin that Wilmot was 'sound' and that it was the editor's role to ensure the history would be unbiased.

He then reluctantly agreed to remove Wilmot from the list. He was troubled by this decision and shared later with Bean that he felt he had compromised his principles by acceding to the prime minister's request.

In an interesting aside, Long records a conversation he had with General Vernon Sturdee in 1946. While discussing the official history, Sturdee asked Long if he had the authority to alter what the writers wrote. Long said that he did, but that he would then expect a writer to record in footnotes that they did not agree with the amendment. Sturdee said he asked this because he thought Wilmot might feel disgruntled and try to get back at Blamey. Long responded that Wilmot probably did feel disgruntled, but that he had too much integrity to do such a thing.

Lionel Wigmore's *The Japanese Thrust* was first published in 1957. Wigmore (1899–1989) joined the staff of the Federal Department of Information in 1939 and then became the department's representative in Singapore in 1941. With the surrender of Singapore imminent in February 1942, he was transferred to Java, where he acted as assistant Australian Government commissioner to the Netherlands East Indies. From 1945 to 1947, he served as a public relations officer with the Australian High Commission, India. His volume, which tackles deeply controversial matters regarding the fall of Singapore, was bound to present him, and Long, with significant challenges. Opinions about the Malaya–Singapore campaigns were deeply divided, and animosity within Army staff ranks continued to seethe, making it almost inevitable that elements of the official history's record of events would provoke unfortunate reactions.

A case in point from the earliest days of the volume's research and consultation was the animosity of General Henry Gordon Bennett, hardly an impartial critic, along with government minister and Bennett supporter Wilfred Kent Hughes. The minister would have gladly brought influence to bear upon the volume if allowed. When consulted, Bennett made unfounded claims of factual inaccuracies, accusing Wigmore of personal bias against him. After much discussion, Long and the British official historian, Stanley Woodburn Kirby, despite some differences of interpretation, reached near unanimity about how to chronicle the Singapore disaster. Their approach, however, has subsequently been criticised (see chapter 11). Australian military historian Professor Peter Stanley, citing the personal and political interests that were being brought to bear on the official history, asserts that 'the difficulty of Wigmore's task should not be underestimated'. It is a credit to the official history team that Wigmore's volume was well received and attracted favourable reviews.

Dudley McCarthy's *South-West Pacific Area First Year – Kokoda to Wau* was first published in 1959. McCarthy (1911–1987) was a school teacher and freelance journalist before enlisting and embarking for the Middle East as a lieutenant with the 2/17th Battalion and then transferring to the headquarters staff of the 6th Division in November 1941. From March 1942, he was back in Australia where he held staff appointments as a temporary major. He worked at the II Corps headquarters in Bougainville in 1944–45. When his AIF service ended, he became an administrative officer with the Universities Commission in Sydney. To test the accuracy of his narrative, McCarthy walked the Kokoda track himself. He acknowledged the Japanese soldiers' 'fighting prowess' and resisted pressure from General Herring to change his assessment of General Allen, whom he described as a 'gallant and capable commander'.[13]

David Dexter's *The New Guinea Offensives* was first published in 1961. Dexter (1917–1992), a school teacher and university-trained historian, enlisted in 1940 and was commissioned in the 2nd Independent Company, later 2/2 Commando Squadron. He served with distinction in Timor and New Guinea, where he was seriously wounded in action, then in Tarakan and Borneo. After returning to Australia in 1946, he accepted Long's invitation to write his volume for the official history at the same time as joining the Department of Foreign Affairs, eventually being appointed as First Secretary with the Australian High Commission in Ceylon and, later, India. He wrote much of his volume while in Ceylon. In the preface to his volume, Dexter revealed how much of a personal, not just a formal, exercise the writing had been for him: 'At many midnights over the years I had perforce to leave Private Smith and his patrol in danger along the jungle track — and yet as often as not I went on with him through the night. To the men who fought, this book is dedicated.'[14]

G Hermon Gill's volumes, *Royal Australian Navy, 1939–1942*, and *Royal Australian Navy, 1942–1945*, were published in 1957 and 1968. Gill (1895–1973) formally accepted the invitation to write his volumes in September 1944, when still serving as a lieutenant commander in the Navy. In October 1945, as Gill ceased his full-time service, Long had several lengthy meetings with him to help get him started. Gill had ready access to documents from the US Navy but was having difficulty getting the British Admiralty to understand the needs of an Australian naval historian. Gill would sit through many meetings attempting to gain access to records that would provide background for his history. He asked for a contract term of six years for his two volumes. Long decided to make it seven. As it turned out, the first volume was not published until 1957, and the second was published in 1968. Gill provided up to 300 000 words for each volume, as stipulated.

Douglas Gillison's *Royal Australian Air Force, 1939–1942* was first published in 1962. Gillison (1899–1965) was a sub-editor of *The Age* from 1937 to 1941, and then of the Melbourne *Argus*. He served as Federal President of the Australian Journalists' Association. During the Second World War, Gillison served with the RAAF and returned to Australia in 1946 with the rank of Squadron Leader to become press secretary to the Minister for Air and subsequently public relations officer for the Department of Civil Aviation. In 1959, he was appointed Director of the Australian News and Information Bureau in London. At the time of his death in 1965, he was Director of Information for P&O Steamship Company. Douglas was the son of Reverend Andrew Gillison, famed for a legendary exploit at Gallipoli in 1915 that cost him his life. Gillison, a member of the 14th Battalion, AIF, volunteered to rescue wounded Anzacs lying helpless in No Man's Land and was cut down by Turkish gunfire.[15] In his volume, Douglas went to considerable effort to include a survey of the beginnings of Australia's development of an Air Force and its involvement in air warfare prior to the Second World War, including the period 1909–1914.

George Odgers' *Air War Against Japan: 1939–1945* was first published in 1957. Odgers (1916–2008), an officer in the RAAF war history section, served as a soldier in the New Guinea and Borneo Campaigns. In 1945, he was commissioned a Flying Officer in the RAAF, serving in Korea, Malaya and Vietnam, retiring with the rank of Group Captain. He was a defence reporter and television news producer in Melbourne during the 1950s and '60s. He outlined the operations of the 5th and 13th American Air Forces with which the RAAF was closely associated in its Pacific campaigns, as well as those of the ground and naval forces. He described planning and command problems, while emphasising the operations and experiences of the Australian squadrons and the crews who flew and serviced the aircraft.[16]

John Herington's *Air War Against Germany and Italy: 1939–1945* and *Air Power Over Europe: 1944–1945* were published in 1954 and 1963. Herington (1916–1967) joined the RAAF in 1941 and served as a pilot with RAF Ferry Command during the war. While flying a Catalina in 1943, he suffered significant injuries in a crash in Ireland and eventually returned to duty as an intelligence officer, then education officer and historian in charge of the historical records section at RAAF Overseas Headquarters, London. Herington's masterly volumes, in which he describes the experience of Australians in air operations over Europe, underpinned by statistical tables showing the relationship of the Australian effort to the total number of sorties, were well received.

Paul Hasluck's *The Government and the People, 1939–1941* and *The Government and the People, 1942–1945* were published in 1952 and 1970. Sir Paul Hasluck (1905–1993), a widely respected figure in academia and public affairs, was recruited into the Department of External Affairs in 1941 but became disillusioned with public policy-making. With the entry of Japan into the war, he remained in Canberra and was assigned as officer-in-charge of postwar policy. Under HV Evatt he worked to formulate the powers of the Commonwealth to oversee postwar reconstruction. He agreed to participate in the official history project in late 1944 but was excused from his contract when he chose to contest the seat of Curtin in the Commonwealth House of

Representatives. Despite his demanding schedule throughout a long and distinguished career in government, foreign affairs and defence policy, including becoming Australia's 17th Governor-General, he continued his writing, as Long put it, 'as a labour of love'.

Sydney Butlin's *War Economy, 1939–1942* was first published in 1955 and co-written with Boris Schedvin, and *War Economy, 1942–1945* was published in 1977. Sydney Butlin (1910–1977) was an economist, historian, statistician and lecturer who wrote *Foundations of the Australian Monetary System 1788–1851* (Melbourne, 1953). During the war, he directed the Economic Division in the Department of War Organisation of Industry. He accepted the invitation to write his volume in August 1943. While tackling his official history volumes, he continued a very influential vocation as Dean of the Economics Faculty at Sydney University.

In addition to his role as official war history writer, Boris Schedvin (1936–2024) was an economist and historian who held various positions, including CSIRO historian, member of the Reserve Bank of Australia Bicentennial Advisory Panel and official historian of the Reserve Bank of Australia. His book *Australia and the Great Depression* (1970) has been widely cited and highly regarded among economists. Schedvin taught or supervised virtually an entire generation of scholars in Australian economic theory.

David Mellor's *The Role of Science and Industry* was published in 1958. Mellor (1903–1980) was a distinguished professor of chemistry. His main research interests were the properties and structures of metal compounds. While working on his official history volume, he was head of the chemistry school at the New South Wales University of Technology. He went on to write books on atomic theory and metal chelates.

Allan Walker's volumes *Clinical Problems of War*, *Middle East and Far East*, *The Island Campaigns* and *Medical Services of the Royal Australian Navy and the Royal Australian Air Force* – with a section on 'Women in the army medical services' – were published in 1952, 1953, 1957 and 1961. When Walker (1887–1958) took over the writing of the medical volumes following the death of Rupert Downes, both he and

Long were dismayed to discover that Downes had been farming out large sections of the history to various writers with specialist expertise and that the first task would involve 'cleaning up this mess'. From there, the work progressed in fits and starts, and the working relationship between Walker and Long continued to deteriorate. Despite the difficulties, the four volumes represent a detailed and highly regarded contribution to the official history.

From notes Long wrote in his diary in July 1947, we gain a glimpse of his tasks as supervisor to the various writers. His projects at that time included, for example, extensive revision of drafts written about Timor, Ambon and New Britain; providing Gillison with a tentative chapter scheme and guiding his research schedule; fretting about the time it was taking McCarthy and Dexter to supply draft chapters; and helping the writers 'to read themselves into' the world in which they were working. He noted with frustration that the 'rate of progress is slower than I had planned'. Lionel Wigmore recalled: 'There were naturally many contrasts between the literary styles and other characteristics of the writers. Many difficulties and differences of opinion or interpretation arose. [Gavin] exercised superb commonsense and almost incredible patience on these as on other occasions.'[17]

As general editor, he took pains to offer detailed advice to writers when needed. He recommended to Dudley McCarthy, for example, that he begin by writing a concise account of no more than 20 000 words as 'a useful trial run for the longer work'. He further suggested that McCarthy develop a disciplined approach to writing, aiming for 2000 words a week, 'doing so much every evening – rain, hail or shine'. He advised him to study examples of good writing, suggesting Bean's *Anzac to Amiens* as a model. He knew from conversations with McCarthy that he was initially daunted by the task. He would need encouragement to 'break the ice' and develop writing habits that were new to him, to 'transfer from the ways of thought and the language of administrative writing'.

Long, meanwhile, regularly updated his style guide for the writers in memoranda or 'circulars', 34 of which he distributed between 1945 and 1953. The circulars included recommended reading and advice on matters of writing style and approach. His attention to detail and practical advice in these circulars give us an insight into his commitment to ensuring the quality, coherence and veracity of the volumes.

Towards the end of 1950, difficulties with Walker were approaching a crisis. In his diaries, Long described Walker as difficult to get on with, wanting better conditions, complaining of non-cooperation from the history project staff, wanting a higher salary, and having sent an 'ultimatum' to the Secretary – presumably of the Public Service Board – setting out terms of conditions and a salary of at least 1750 pounds. Long was stung by this memo. 'Taken at face value the memo leaves me branded as quite inefficient and unsympathetic and demands a formal affirmation of conditions most of which I have already tried to apply.'[18] Despite these trying and rather personal frictions, Long made a point of travelling to Sydney with Bill Sweeting in September 1956 to visit Walker – who, by that time, was gravely ill in hospital – to offer support to Walker's wife and to inquire if she needed financial assistance. Long and Bean had discussed seeking a literary fund pension for Walker. He died in January 1958.

Few people knew at the time that Gavin was living with considerable pain, having undergone ten days of deep X-ray therapy for sciatica in March of the previous year. The X-rays of his lumbosacral spine showed no evidence of malignancy but revealed marked disk degeneration and spondylolisthesis. He had feared around that time that he may have the early symptoms of Hodgkin's disease. By the end of 1958, with 11 official history volumes published and the others well in hand, Gavin Long, struggling with daily discomfort and exhaustion, notified the writers and staff that he planned his partial or complete retirement 'in about three years'. He soldiered on until 1963 when, as Wigmore put it, 'he dismissed himself when the work had reached a stage where he considered it no longer justified his full-time employment.'[19]

The brief years that followed afforded Gavin Long an opportunity to turn his attention to other writing projects and speaking engagements, continue his work on the AWM Board and spend more time in his Canberra home with Jocelyn and his extended families of the Longs and the Brittens.

# 11
# CRITICISMS OF GAVIN LONG AND THE OFFICIAL HISTORY

*... his task as an official historian was so immense that it could not have been completed ... without there being some gaps.*

– Robert O'Neill[1]

How are we to assess the quality of Gavin Long's official history? Can historians be confident that it is trustworthy? And against what criteria might criticisms be judged?

It is, perhaps, more within the scope of an academic treatise than a general biography to adequately assess the legacy of Long's official history. Yet some things are clear. Given his authorship and close personal oversight of the project, any accusations of error or inadequacy may be assessed in light of what is known of his character and skill as a historian and writer, and with reference to his stated aims and objectives. It is telling that very little published criticism of the official history is to be found; however, four topics bear scrutiny.

First, the official history fails to provide a comprehensive account of Australian POWs. From the outset, Gavin Long was aware of the need, as he reminded Prime Minister Curtin, to interview returned POWs to compile a rounded narrative. Notwithstanding the three excellent chapters in Lionel Wigmore's volume *The Japanese Thrust* (as discussed in chapter 6) chronicling the plight of Japanese POWs and its appendix listing 18 books by Australian prisoners of the Japanese, the criticism stands. Where in the official history is a comprehensive treatment of the experiences of Australian POWs in all theatres between 1940 and 1945? It is easy to conclude that the topic was not covered satisfactorily.

Second, Professor Peter Stanley has criticised Lionel Wigmore's *The Japanese Thrust* for the scant attention paid to the well-documented and criminal behaviour by some Australian soldiers fleeing the Japanese as Singapore fell – including desertion, looting, rape and even murder.

Throughout January and February 1942, the Japanese attacked aggressively down the Malay Peninsula towards Singapore, which they reached on 31 January, causing panic and confusion among the ill-prepared and ill-equipped British, Indian and Australian defenders. For many in Britain and Australia, Singapore had been touted as a 'fortress', capable of repelling any seaborne attack. It came as a shock to many when, by 14 February, the Japanese had captured Singapore's reservoirs and pumping stations and it was clear they could not be stopped. Lieutenant General Arthur Percival, the British commander in Singapore, announced that the Allied forces would capitulate on 15 February. Australia's commanding officer, Lieutenant General Gordon Bennett, had already escaped from Singapore, for which he was later severely criticised. When Winston Churchill heard that Singapore had fallen, he called it the 'worst disaster' in British military history, and news of the defeat reverberated ominously throughout a stunned Australia.

Wigmore's volume chronicling the Malaya/Singapore campaign was first published in 1957. The relevant chapters are contained in Part II of the volume: 'South-East Asia conquered'. It has been noted that Wigmore's task was unavoidably fraught. He was researching, writing and publishing the history of the fall of Singapore in the immediate aftermath of the war when the effects of the deeply traumatic and, in some cases, shameful events must have been widely known and keenly felt by the survivors. The saga as it unfolded was controversial at almost every level, deeply humiliating for the British and Australian armed forces, and terrifying for the Australian population, which suddenly felt exposed and defenceless in the face of a seemingly unstoppable Japanese onslaught. In sifting through the evidence and assembling a narrative, the editor and writer of this part of the official history were dealing with deeply troubling, offensive and painful facts. Producing a fair, accurate and complete narrative demanded rigour, integrity and courage.

British General Archibald Wavell, the British regional commander in the Far East during the campaign, submitted a report to Churchill immediately after the fall of Singapore, which remained subject to British official secrets legislation for 50 years. It was made public in January 1993 and British newspapers began reporting Wavell's contention that the Australians were responsible for the defeat. A diplomatic furore ensued in Australia, but researchers, notably Dr Peter Elphick, were now able to begin digging into previously unavailable official files. The facts they yielded were damning. In light of what is now on the record, it is clear that Wigmore's volume, while an admirable account of the larger campaign, was not an adequate account of Australian desertions and crimes in Singapore.

In his 1995 book *Singapore: The Pregnable Fortress: A Study in Deception, Discord and Desertion*, Elphick dismissed Wavell's accusation that the Australians were to blame as 'unacceptable as it stands' given the wider and more complicated combination of factors at play at the time. However, he demonstrates that the essential facts about the desertions, 'of which the Australians were a substantial part', did shorten the siege of Singapore and blacken the name of the Australian Army. Elphick has assembled a well-documented account of widespread desertion, looting, rape and murder on the part of Australians, starkly concluding that Singapore represents 'the highest incidence of desertion from any army, anywhere at any time'.[2]

Why was this not all made plain in the official history? Elphick's conclusion about Wigmore's volume is that when Churchill returned to office in 1951, much of the compiling of official histories about the Malayan campaign in Australia and Britain was well underway. A study of the documentation in the British National Archives from that time 'leaves the reader with the impression that the two sets of historians were as much interested in coming to a consensus on *how to present the story* [emphasis added] as they were in documenting what had happened'. British official historian Woodburn Kirby visited Australia in 1953 to find such a consensus. While there, he and Wigmore interviewed officers, gathering new information and finding 'a consensus of presentation', resulting in both the British and Australian histories giving scant attention to the matter of Australian desertions.[3] This represented only one of many cover-ups that are now evident. Kirby 'was definitely under some constraints'. Elphick does not mention Long's role in Wigmore's history, but we have seen that Long had such a close and active involvement in the project that he is clearly implicated in any editorial failures.

In 1956, the Australian Chief of Staff in Malaya, Colonel JH Thyer, wrote to General Percival, declaring that any watering down 'does not worry me, as a discerning person would read between the lines'. It may not have been a concern for Thyer, but it is definitely a concern for historians.

Wavell claimed his report to Churchill was 'fair and accurate'. Is the Australian official history fair and accurate? In Wigmore's volume, all references to desertion are found in chapter 17, 'Cease Fire', and relate to the increasing chaos between 9 and 19 February. Describing the events of 14 February, Wigmore notes that groups of armed soldiers, including Australians, were 'at large, seeking escape' and were reported to have demanded to be boarded on small vessels embarking evacuating non-combatants, even firing upon such vessels. Wigmore describes an increasingly desperate state of mind in many of the Australians and offers that some of them may have been driven to extreme acts by a concern that their homeland would be exposed if they were all captured by the Japanese and prevented from taking part in future fighting. Being aware that they would be unable to defend their own soil was perhaps 'their bitterest thought', wrote Wigmore. It is easy to conclude that Wigmore erred in attempting to mitigate their culpability, couching a brief reference to odious actions and then immediately offering a psychological rationale for them. It does no justice to anyone. The reader is presented with a glimpse of the stark facts about the shambles the Australian soldiers lived through that day, but it remains unenlightened about the extent of the unconscionable behaviour.

Wigmore rightly differentiates between 'escapers' and 'deserters'. For Wigmore, escapers were those who were being evacuated from Singapore and those who escaped after Singapore fell. Deserters, on the other hand, were those who fled or detached themselves from their units during hostilities. He admits that the distinction between these categories is sometimes difficult to draw clearly. And in light of the widespread rumour on the island early on 15 February that a ceasefire would come into effect at 4:30 pm that day, the conclusion inferred is that anyone who acted upon the rumour was acting 'in good faith' and may not be considered a deserter.

Yet, Wigmore does acknowledge that the behaviour of some Australian soldiers 'blackened the reputation of their fellow countrymen'. He provides the example of a Dutch-Javanese police officer whose hospitality towards a party of 12 Australian soldiers was met with acts of theft and vandalism. Yet it is undeniable that the reader is not presented with the full story. According to Elphick, Australian deserters totalled more than 8000 men – close to half of the Australian troops there.[4]

These facts were surely available to the official history researchers. Elphick cites many documents and there were many eyewitnesses who might have been interviewed. The question at hand is whether a full and accurate depiction of the shameful episode is evident in the official history. Clearly, it is not.

It might be argued that the wider Australian community may also be complicit in this failure. There has long been a reluctance to confront the harsh realities. In an interview with Fairfax journalist Lindsay Murdoch in 2012, Peter Stanley, referring to the abiding misconceptions about Allied attempts to repel the Japanese offensive at Singapore, ventured:

> Australians will probably continue to be sensitive about it until well after the last veterans are dead and possibly even after their children are dead. There is a very strong sympathy for the World War II veterans – they are regarded as national treasures to be cherished. So while they are alive they will not be talking about Singapore in an impartial way.[5]

Yet, this alleged reluctance to face facts does not absolve the official historian of the responsibility to fully present them.

How can Long's oversight of such narratives in the official history be accounted for? In an address to an international conference of historians in Singapore in 2002, Peter Stanley described Gavin Long's approach to the chronicling of the Malaya–Singapore campaign as one of 'discretion rather than risky candour'.[6] While this is shrewd, it seems generous. There is no evidence of cowardice, carelessness or duplicity anywhere else in Gavin Long's life or work. Quite the contrary. He consistently demonstrated integrity, determination and courage and was deeply respected by those who knew him well. As a historian, he consistently showed a commitment to sober and detailed accuracy. Yet Long was a fallible human being. Perhaps he was guilty in this instance of an error of judgment, electing to 'pull the punch' for reasons we cannot know with certainty. If so, it was indeed an error. Risky candour is surely an essential requirement for the historian, and more so for a nation's official historian.

A third criticism of the official history concerns Long's account of the Battle of Bardia. Australian military historian and current official historian Professor Craig Stockings has criticised Gavin Long's account of the Battle of Bardia, accusing him of failing to accurately interpret and assess strategic and tactical elements of the battle. Stockings acknowledges Long's superb legacy in other respects and posits that Long may have been captive to the so-called 'Anzac myth'.

The first battle fought by the Australians in the Second World War was against the Italian garrison at Bardia in North Africa between 3 and 5 January 1941. The account of the battle, found in Long's *To Benghazi*, was his first as official historian. It has served as the foundation for all subsequent knowledge of that episode and has been generally well regarded. Stockings' critique of Long's account is twofold. First, that it perpetuates an error embraced by a long line of Australian military historians who have dismissed the Italians as inherently inept and cowardly. Second, that Long and subsequent historians have disproportionately credited the Allied victory at Bardia to the infantry, exacerbating the Anzac mythology that Australian soldiers are inherently superior in battle.

In 2009, Stockings wrote: 'In an otherwise comprehensive and excellent account, Long perpetuated many of the misguided wartime interpretations of Bardia'.[7] He then elaborated, somewhat puzzled by

Long's approach, that he was 'well aware that at the time of writing there were still sufficient survivors left to challenge his position'.[8]

Did Gavin Long 'perpetrate misguided interpretations', knowingly sacrificing good history on the altar of a false god – the myth of the superior Anzac? If so, Long's reputation as official historian is damaged.[9] To respond to Stockings' criticisms, it is important to differentiate Long, the wartime journalist, from Long, the historian. Then it is necessary to scrutinise his analysis in the two chapters he devotes to the Battle of Bardia in *To Benghazi*. It becomes clear there are inadequacies in Long's analysis, but these are not fatal to his integrity and competence.

Craig Stockings rightly differentiates between Long, the wartime newspaperman, and Long, the official historian. The project of the newspaperman is not that of the historian. As a wartime correspondent, Long reported events day to day, relying on limited available information and under editorial oversight and censorship. He was limited by the strictures of column inches and mindful of the importance of morale in the population. The use of colourful and jingoistic language suited the paper's general readership. Once in the role of general editor of the official history, however, he was required to apply the sober, measured style of the historian.

In an example cited by Stockings, Long's report in the *Sydney Morning Herald* in January 1941, 'NSW battalions chosen for assault', described the spectacular success of the infantry assault on the garrison, supported by tanks, artillery, and naval and aerial bombardment. He reported that the Italian soldiers were suffering from hunger and lack of transport and supply, and were ready to surrender. Yet, the reader cannot help but be left with a glowing regard for the Australian infantryman and the sense that the 'little' Italian man had been all too keen to surrender: 'The Italians just threw up their hands. It seemed as if they had white flags all ready.'[10] An ethnocentric explanation for the Italians fighting so poorly, 'the image of physically weak, cowardly, even effeminate Italian soldiers', was promulgated not just by Gavin Long, but also his fellow Australian war correspondents such as Chester Wilmot, John Hetherington and Alan Moorehead.[11] Stockings agrees that examples like this are not admissible as evidence in any accusation that Long failed as a historian. After all, that's what newspapermen were expected and encouraged to do. 'What is far less excusable was the ease with which postwar authors and historians accepted and propagated these types of explanations.'[12]

Stockings asserts that there has been a long line of military commentators and historians who continued the pattern and legitimised the misrepresented tradition, the idea of intrinsic Italian cowardice and innate Italian military ineffectiveness. To what extent, however, can a flawed approach by future writers be laid at the feet of Gavin Long, the historian?

Stockings asserts that Long's conclusions are seriously undermined by *his determination* not to break the Anzac tradition of making Australian infantrymen the key determinant of victory. 'Long was unequivocal', Stockings declares, 'that the decisive work at Bardia was done by ingenious and resolute foot soldiers', thus reprising Bean's depiction of the primacy of Australian infantrymen on the battlefield.[13] Long's claims about the decisive contribution of infantry at Bardia are, indeed, open to criticism by military strategists. His interpretations are necessarily subjective to a degree. His motivations, however, are ultimately less certain. Was he, by nature, overly sympathetic towards the infantryman, almost to the point of sycophancy? And if so, was it because he was captive to a myth? He certainly cannot be accused of this in the light of his total body of work, but perhaps in this instance he can.

Stockings casts further suspicion on Long's motivations by pointing to his declaration that the objective of Australian war histories is 'nationalistic'. In an address to the Australia and New Zealand Association for the Advancement of Science in 1954, Long conceded that 'the one objective of the Australian war histories is frankly a nationalistic one – to contribute to the statement of a national tradition'.[14] Yet, given all that can be known about Gavin Long, it is reasonable to conclude that what he meant was that 'the smaller partners in coalition wars must write their own stories if they wish them to be told in reasonable detail'.[15] This is not necessarily the same as perpetrating a myth or beating a nationalistic drum.

As Long's was the first official account, drawn from all available sources, it did establish an *interpretation* of what occurred at Bardia. While it is true that the battle was as huge a success for General Mackay as it was a humiliating defeat for General Annibale Bergonzoli, any conclusions drawn about the intrinsic inferiority of Italians are inexcusably false. Subsequent authors may well have developed interpretations of their own, but these are not Long's responsibility unless the foundation he laid is so flawed that future writers were never going to be able to construct a sound and true narrative. So is the foundation fatally flawed? Are its interpretations seriously misguided, as Stockings asserts?

Stockings' analysis of the battle highlights four advantages possessed by the Allies that contributed to the Italian defeat, none of which, he convincingly points out, have to do with ethnic inferiority or cowardice: logistics, weapons and tactics, the role of air and sea power, and leadership and training.

Is Long's account an accurate treatment of these strategic and tactical factors? And, equally importantly, is the reader left with the erroneous impression that 'the Anzacs won because they were Anzacs'?[16]

Gavin Long's 44-page chapter 'The Battle of Bardia' is preceded by a 20-page chapter describing the preparations that were made in the period between 14 December 1940 and the assault of 2 January 1941. Thus, Long devotes 64 pages to his description of the battle, ending with a 3-page analysis as a postscript. Long's analytical summary is instructive.

In his summary, he notes that General O'Connor wagered heavily on the lack of spirit and proven inefficiency of the Italians, but that the Australians' task would have 'tested the keenest and most experienced troops'.[17] This is a recognition of both the advantages the Allies possessed in training and morale and the formidable opposition that nevertheless could be expected from the defenders. There is no imputation of inherent cowardice on the one side, or prowess on the other. Further, after the battle, 'some Australian senior officers' who had served in the First AIF in France, but who had not been present at

Bardia, made light of the Italian defence and worried that the victory would leave the Australians unrealistically cocky. To this, Long replies, 'but the Italians fought hard'.

The Australian senior commanders were drawn from men who experienced the Great War and 'in almost every platoon were men whose fathers had served in the old AIF and were resolved to show themselves at least as formidable as their fathers'. The troops had great admiration for the veteran commanders who had schooled them in the kind of aggressive patrolling in which the old force had excelled and in 'the doctrine that battles are won by attacking'. If Long's assessment is correct, it might be argued that Anzac prowess in this instance arose not from a mythical inherent ethnic superiority but from a morale-stiffening ambition to live up to profound expectations.

Stockings makes a strong case when critiquing Long's overemphasis on the role of Australian infantry at the battle. Long acknowledged that prior to this battle, there was widespread agreement that well-fortified positions supported by rapid-fire weapons were all but impregnable, and that mobile armour and air power were needed to give attackers greater superiority. He then inexplicably concludes that at Bardia, however, 'the decisive work was done by ingenious and resolute foot soldiers moving close behind an artillery barrage'. In a footnote, Long tempers the claim that British tanks had won the day, citing Wavell's despatch in which he asserted that the tanks relied heavily on 'the bold employment of infantry both in the assault and in the exploitation'.[18]

Criticism of Long's tactical analysis here is warranted. And it is a fair explanation for his faulty analysis that he had an overly sympathetic mindset towards the primacy of infantry in general and was convinced of the superior quality of Australian infantry in particular. It is less fair to criticise Long for knowingly perpetrating a myth.

A final criticism relates to Long's chronicling of the Southwest Pacific campaigns fought by Australia during 1944 and 1945 in his volume *The Final Campaigns*. It arises from the longstanding debates and controversies labelling the campaigns unnecessary, resulting in the loss of thousands of Australian lives for political rather than military ends.[19] The legitimacy of the battles was debated in Parliament throughout 1945. Newspapers reported the debates and senior soldiers expressed opinions. Peter Charlton makes the case in his 1983 book *The Unnecessary War: Island Campaigns of the South-West Pacific 1944–45* that the campaigns were fought more for the self-aggrandisement of generals than to achieve sound, strategic objectives.

Did Gavin Long gloss over or conceal legitimate claims that the New Guinea and Bougainville campaigns were unnecessary? Peter Charlton levels no such criticism directly at Long. Rather, he draws heavily from and 'highly recommends' Long's detailed accounts in *The Final Campaigns*.[20] Indeed, Long's volume is superb and the reader is left in no doubt. In his preface, Long declares that the various operations of 1945 were 'strategically of minor importance', and scattered throughout the narratives he reminds the reader of the tensions that were at play at the time. For example, 'the losses suffered by the Australians were made harder to bear by reason of the conviction, particularly among veteran campaigners, that the operations were of minor importance',[21] and 'during the exacting fighting of February, March and April, Australian troops became increasingly convinced that the campaign was not worth their blood and sweat',[22] and 'despite losses, weariness and the nagging conviction that the campaign was not worthwhile, the men retained their pride in themselves'.[23]

Long devoted the first five chapters of his volume to a comprehensively researched and eminently readable summary of the political, military and societal forces at play during the months between September 1944 and August 1945. Describing the international political exigencies, the strategic and tactical challenges, and the effects of clashing command personalities, he leaves the reader with an appreciation of the complexities and contradictions that, perhaps inevitably, led to campaigns susceptible to the accusation of 'unnecessary'. No criticism of Gavin Long's account holds in this regard. In his own words:

> When the chronicler has described the events and their outcome and set out the opinions of those who bore the responsibility of it, he is perhaps justified in feeling diffident about adding to those

> opinions an opinion of his own, his own inclinations having been given sufficient latitude in his selection and presentation of evidence and contemporary opinion.[24]

Robert O'Neill's assertion that Gavin Long's task as an official historian was so immense that it could not have been completed without some gaps would seem self-evident. The fair-minded reader and student of history can judge the official history against Long's stated aims and priorities for the project and confidently conclude that his history stands as a monumental, reliable and trustworthy achievement. Along with Bean's, his history has won high praise internationally and, more important, 'a generation of scholars has been satisfied' with what it contains.[25]

# Epilogue
# HIS FINAL CAMPAIGNS

In April 1968, Fairfax journalist Bruce Juddery spoke with Gavin Long in his home. The interview led to a piece published in the *Canberra Times* entitled 'War expert drops hint'.

'The interior of Gavin Long's Deakin home is very English in a solid, brown way', Juddery wrote. 'There are a great many shelves of books, few of them paperbacks, and comfortable, uncontemporary furniture; in the sitting room, there is a large late-Victorian portrait of a woman and a big leather pouffe. It all suggests an Anglican minister more readily than a pioneer defence journalist.'[1] Juddery quipped that Gavin more closely resembled the stereotypical parson than did his bishop father, describing George as 'an advanced-thinking ecumenist with the presence of the brisk administrator'. He was struck by Gavin's gaunt frame, noting that he had been 'reduced by a recent illness to a stone below his normal weight'.

It seems that the 'hint' Juddery felt Long was dropping in the course of their conversation related to Long's concern that Australia was misguided to pursue aggressive policies towards East Asia, particularly Vietnam. Regarding that conflict, he said:

> I think the days of Western bridgeheads in Asia are almost over. We should support those who are seeking settlement in Vietnam even if it means loss of face and even at the risk of it leading finally to a united Vietnam under Ho Chi Minh – a sort of East Asian Yugoslavia.

Long felt that a more pressing concern was the possibility of American or Japanese interests overtaking Australian manufacturing and industry. Of particular concern was the potential for a return to government policies that left Australia too dependent on Allies for its military preparedness.

Long had been made an Officer of the British Empire in 1953 and awarded the Gold Cross of the Royal Order of the Phoenix by King Paul of Greece in 1956 for 'promoting Greece's stature abroad' through his journalistic and historical contributions. In 1959, he completed his third volume in the official history series, *The Final Campaigns*. He told Juddery that he retired from the project in 1963 'not because I was finished but because I felt a full-time General Editor was no longer required'. He added that he had as much work in front of him as he could cope with. Never content to sit idle, retirement was an opportunity for him to devote his remaining time and energy to what may be described as his final campaigns.

Gavin's mother died in October of the previous year, aged 85, and he was named as executor of her will, a responsibility he discharged with his customary thoroughness. He continued on the AWM Board of Trustees, a position he had held since 1943, as the AWM's principal adviser on history and films, and an initiator of its research scholarship and grants programmes. He became a Research Fellow at the Australian National University. He added to these responsibilities the role of Assistant Editor of the Australian Dictionary of Biography. He became a regular contributor to *Stand-To* journal, providing many reviews and occasional papers for publication. He was a prolific contributor to the *Canberra Times*, contributing over 90 articles and book reviews.

In 1963, *The Final Campaigns* was published. More than six decades later, the interested reader who comes with no prior knowledge of Australia's involvement in the war of 1939–1945, unsure where to begin, would do well to read the final chapter of this volume, 'Looking back', which is succinct, deeply informed and vividly written.

In 1966, Long was commissioned to co-author a style manual for Commonwealth government publications, and in May of that year, attended a meeting at Crawford Television Productions in Melbourne on behalf of the AWM to discuss a proposed colour film about the AWM. He had been asked, along with JD Howse, to assist Douglas Tainsh with the writing of the television script 'He is here'. A copy of this 32-minute, 16-millimetre film is available from the AWM.[2]

At the beginning of the school year in 1967, in a development we can only imagine Long would have found gratifying, All Saints' College, Bathurst began dividing the student body into three houses – Bean, Bishop and Long. Meanwhile, he continued to finalise the manuscript for *MacArthur as Military Commander*, his biography of General Douglas MacArthur, published in 1969. He also continued to work on his one-volume version of the official history, *The Six Years War: A Concise History of Australia in the 1939–1945 War*, published in late 1973.

At the time of its publication, Long's *MacArthur*, the first serious biography of that general written by an Australian, was reviewed in a *Canberra Times* article by Manning Clark.[3] Clark wrote:

> In finding such a biographer as Gavin Long, MacArthur was most certainly a very lucky man: for Long could mourn the man's grandeur of spirit, and not mock at his errors. Perhaps his greatest piece of luck was to have a man of such warmth and tenderness and sympathy as Gavin Long to leave for posterity a very distinguished biography of all his struts and frets on the stage of human history.

By way of example of MacArthur's 'luck', Long's biography concludes:

> his desire for adulation made him prey to devoted followers who flattered his conviction that he was infallible and that people in Washington were conspiring against him. But this was a minor, though damaging foible measured against his other qualities: his courage, his patriotism, his ability to inspire his subordinates and others, including anxious Australians in 1942.

*The Six Years War* was reviewed in considerable detail by the official historian of Australia in the Korean War, Professor Robert O'Neill, in *Historical Studies*.[4] O'Neill highlighted and broadly approved Long's emphasis in the single volume on Army operations over those of the Navy and the RAAF. He noted that Long was unflinching in his critiques of the performance of Australian politicians, including Menzies' complacency and Curtin's demeaning sycophancy before the United States, asserting that the Australian Government under both prime ministers 'had made a notable surrender of sovereignty'. He concluded that the reader is well served by Long's very clear tactical analyses, while his sketchy assessments of the effects of the character of Australia's military leaders are 'less than satisfying'. While he provided only brief treatments of Australian military leaders, 'Long does not spare General Douglas MacArthur', exposing MacArthur not as a military incompetent but as a man whose preoccupations with his own position continually masked many of the better qualities in his nature. 'Throughout the volume, Long keeps his readers' feet on economic terra firma by discussion of the limiting effect of the economy upon the size and scope of Australia's military operations.'[5]

Gavin Long's final campaign ended on 10 October 1968 after a battle with cancer. At the time of his death, he had seen all of the official history published, except the final *War Economy* volume. The family farewelled him in a private cremation in Canberra on 11 October. The death notice was succinct: 'Long, Gavin Merrick, husband of Jocelyn, father of Jenifer and Jeremy, father-in-law of Frances, grand-father of Daniel, Adam and Benjamin'.[6]

Bill Sweeting described Long's final months in his memoir:

> Gavin died not long after Dr Bean, rousing himself from his sickbed to compose a tribute to his predecessor for a newspaper. I saw him often in those last days, when he was confined to bed and struggling to finish his book on MacArthur. He was sedated against discomfort and pain – he once described discomfort, as when he was unable to sleep at night; pain, as when he had to bite his lips to stop himself from screaming – and he used to apologise for his inability at times to immediately grasp the import of what I was trying to tell him.[7]

On 8 May 1970, the *Canberra Times* reported that a scholarship was to be awarded annually at All Saints' College, Bathurst in memory of the late Gavin Long.[8] The scholarship fund was raised by an AWM committee headed by Lieutenant General Edmund Herring. The committee announced that $500 would be awarded annually to a student in their fifth and sixth year at All Saints' College. That same year, with the encouragement and assistance of Bill Sweeting, who supplied photographs, South Australian sculptor John Stuart Dowie completed a bronze bust of Long for display in the AWM galleries. Unsurprisingly, Long himself had rejected a suggestion a few years earlier that his portrait be painted for the AWM collection. For many years, the bust stood alongside Charles Bean's, flanking the public entrance to the AWM in a fitting acknowledgment of the profound contribution of these two men to Australian military history. The bust has since been removed from public display and, despite attempts by this author to have it replaced, it remains locked away in the AWM vaults.

On 21 August 1973, Stuart Sayers, author of *Ned Herring*, wrote to Herring, who was then chairman of the Board of AWM Trustees, requesting consideration be given to publishing Long's diaries. Some consideration was given to the proposal, but the minutes of the AWM Literary and Films Committee from 24 April 1975 reveal that Bill Sweeting, then acting director, had received correspondence from Ian Fitchett, who had been asked to look into it. Fitchett recommended against publication. Sweeting added, 'his opinion against publication was based a great deal on the fear that he might be asked to edit the diaries'.[9]

Gavin Long's success and that of his official history team may be gauged against his own stated objectives. He wanted the interested general public to find the work intelligible, informative and satisfying. He wanted the reader to understand and appreciate the experiences of the men and women in the thick of battle. He wanted the narratives to unfold as if in real time so that the reader would be carried along by the story, not just observe dispassionately from a future vantage point. He wanted the accounts to be as fair as possible to all parties concerned. Finally, he wanted the work to accurately tell the national story in its global context. Readers and students today are left to judge the work by these broad objectives.

In his review of *The Six Years War*, Robert O'Neill concluded that both Bean's and Long's histories 'have won high praise internationally and, more important, a generation of scholars using them have been satisfied with what they contain'.[10]

Long consistently proved himself worthy of Charles Bean's unflinching endorsement. It seems impossible to find a single serious criticism of Gavin Long's character, and the few criticisms that may be directed at the official history actually serve to highlight the overall quality of the work. A good and decent man, he embodied to the end Bean's twin ideals of 'capacity and character'. He brought impressive skill and relentless determination to the task. His team admired and loved him, and the quality of their work is testament to his leadership. His sublime combination of personal integrity, disciplined intelligence and seemingly boundless energy owed much to his late father's influence, his mentor's advice and his wife's sustaining support and companionship.

He was not without his biases and 'blind spots' and, if anything, could be accused of being too humble. Yet, his humility was both a strength and a weakness. It gave rise to his staunch advocacy of the ordinary soldier, alongside whom he felt himself a 'lesser being'. On behalf of the soldiers, he did not hesitate to criticise poor military leadership, encourage better conditions and, of course, pour out his energy and talent to ensure their stories were properly told. On the other hand, this very humility may have sometimes contributed to a somewhat overawed attitude towards service personnel, especially infantrymen. From his youth at All Saints', in the shadow of his ebullient and widely admired father who went off to war, he was influenced by his gentle and inspirational teacher, Mr Brown, who served in the First World War, and his school chums, who also went off to war, some of them never to return.

Gavin Long's biographer may be forgiven for concluding that the man was too self-effacing – eschewing his own importance, reluctant to be in the limelight and restricting himself to project-related diaries, which provide mere glimpses into his personal thoughts and feelings. He never bothered to maintain a personal diary. The inner man is discernible only by inference from his works, although it must be added that Gavin was a diligent writer of newsy, affectionate, engaging letters and postcards to his family.

It is impossible to guess how he would have written his own epitaph, but he would have considered it unseemly to even contemplate it. We can only intuit how he felt about his professional contribution as a journalist and war correspondent, his many publications or the official history. As for his feelings as a father and husband, as a son and brother, we have evidence of his love and devotion to Jocie and his proud affection for his children in his letters to them and, perhaps more importantly, in their enduring love, affection and respect for him.

For soldiers like Claudie and Bernie Damm and the Australians caught up in the cataclysm of the Second World War, Gavin Long's legacy is an immense and enduring body of work that continues to be an essential and trustworthy resource for historians, and a priceless gift to the nation.

# ACKNOWLEDGMENTS

This project would have foundered at many points had it not been for Professor Peter Stanley, to whom I am deeply indebted for his wise and generous guidance since its inception. It was Peter who introduced me to Gavin Long's unsung legacy in such a way that I felt compelled to find out more about this impressive, enigmatic man, and introduce him to his own country where, until now, he has remained largely unknown. Having guided the project to completion, it was Peter who then offered invaluable assistance in getting the work published. I am sincerely grateful for the generous advice and encouragement of Dr Michael McKernan. Conversations with Michael helped me as I grappled with a number of questions about Long's methodology and also shed light on some of the people at the Australian War Memorial who Long worked with.

Professor Craig Stockings stimulated my quest to dig deeper into the motivations, strengths and weaknesses of Gavin Long's approach. Craig's perspectives as an official historian himself were most helpful. Dr Peter Dennis provided much-needed insight into Long's relationships with various key military historians in the United States. Tammy Pemper and Ian Campbell provided valuable writing advice, and Ian ensured my manuscript was fit to present to a publisher. I am grateful to Emily Hyles for her diligent and talented research assistance, and I have appreciated the helpful staff at the War Memorial Research Centre. Gavin's son, Jeremy, and grandson, Daniel, have been generous in providing family papers and anecdotes. The Army History Unit, who appreciate the crucial role Gavin Long has played in our wartime history, generously provided a grant that enabled me to travel to the Australian War Memorial Research Centre and National Library in Canberra.

I am deeply grateful to Elspeth Menzies, Paul O'Beirne, Gabriella Sterio and the team at NewSouth Publishing for immediately seeing the importance of telling Gavin Long's story, for having confidence in me to tell it, and for their hard work and expertise in helping me bring it to fruition.

Finally, I acknowledge the unstinting support, encouragement and interest of my family and their belief in me.

# BIBLIOGRAPHY

**Articles and books**


Barker, T, *A History of Bathurst, Vol. 2: From Settlement to City*, Bathurst City Council, Bathhurst,1998.

Bazley, A, 'Obituary: C.E.W. Bean', *Historical Studies*, vol. 14, no. 53, October 1969, p. 147.

Bean, CEW, *Flagships Three*, Hodder & Stoughton, London, 1916.

—— 'Sidelights of the war on Australian character', *Journal of the Royal Australian Historical Society*, vol. 13, pt. 4, 1927, pp. 209–223.

—— 'The writing of the Australian official history of the Great War – Sources, methods and some conclusions', *Royal Australian Historical Society Journal and Proceedings*, vol. 14, part 2, Sydney, 1938, pp. 85–113.

—— *The A.I.F. in France*, Australian War Memorial, Canberra, 1942.

—— 'Our war history', *Bulletin*, 27 May 1942, p. 2.

—— 'The technique of a contemporary war historian', *Australian Historical Studies*, 2:6, 1942, pp. 65–79.

Bridge, C, 'Anglo-Australian attitudes: Remembering and re-reading Russell Ward', *Journal of Australian Colonial History*, vol. 10, no. 2, 2008, pp. 187–200.

Charlton, P, *The Unnecessary War: Island Campaigns of the South-West Pacific 1944–45*, Macmillan, Melbourne, 1983.

Clark, M, 'Honour, duty and errors', *Canberra Times*, 16 August 1969, p. 13.

Dexter, D, *The New Guinea Offensives*, Australian War Memorial, Canberra, 1961.

Ellis, Major LF, *The War in France and Flanders 1939–1940*, United Kingdom Military, HMSO, London, 1954.

Elphick, P, *Singapore: The Pregnable Fortress: A Study in Deception, Discord and Desertion*, Hodder & Stoughton, London, 1995.

Gillison, D, *Royal Australian Air Force, 1939–1942*, Australian War Memorial, Canberra, 1962.

Gorman, E, 'The glory that is Greece', *Brisbane Truth*, 26 August 1942, p. 6.

Grehan, J & Mace, M, *The BEF in France 1939–1940: Manning the Front Through to the Dunkirk Evacuation*, Pen & Sword, Barnsley, 2014.

Grey, J, 'War correspondents', *Australian Book Review*, June 1999, p. 10.

—— *A Military History of Australia*, Cambridge University Press, Cambridge, 1999.

Griffen-Foley, B (ed.), *A Companion to the Australian Media*, Australian Scholarly Publishing, Kew, 2014.

Hasluck, P, *The Government and the People, 1939–1941*, Australian War Memorial, Canberra, [1952]1965.

Herington, J, *Air War Against Germany and Italy 1939–1943*, Australian War Memorial, Canberra, 1954.

Hermon Gill, G, *Royal Australian Navy, 1942–1945*, Australian War Memorial, Canberra, 1968.

—— 'War historian Gavin Long dead', *The Age*, 11 October 1968, p. 6.

Hetherington, J, 'Australian file: Gavin Long', *The Age*, 12 November 1960.

—— *Forty-Two Faces: Profiles of Living Australian Writers*, FW Cheshire, Melbourne, 1962.

Horner, D, 'The evolution of Australian official war histories', in D Marston & T Leahy (eds.), *War, Strategy and History: Essays in Honour of Professor Robert O'Neill*, ANU Press, Canberra, 2016, pp. 73–90.

Jamieson, S, 'Gavin Long – An appreciation', *The Bathurstian: The Magazine of All Saints' College Bathurst*, All Saints' College, Bathurst, 1968.

Johnson, WH, *The Right Reverend George Merrick Long, Lord Bishop of Bathurst 1911–1928, Lord Bishop of Newcastle 1928–1930: A Memoir*, St John's College Press, Morpeth, 1930.

Juddery, B, 'War expert drops hint', *Canberra Times*, 24 April 1968, p. 18.

Kerr, D, 'Bardia: Myth, reality and the heirs of ANZAC', *Australian Army Journal*, vol. 7, no. 2, 2010, pp. 139–144.

Koziol, M, 'Don't mention the war: Why Canberra suppresses the story of East Timor', *Sydney Morning Herald*, 24 November 2019.

Long, G, 'Record-breaking in the fifties: Prodigious feats of the Flying Pieman', *Argus*, 27 September 1930, p. 2.

—— 'A layman's complaint', *Art in Australia*, no. 42, February 1932, pp. 20–22.

—— 'Some paintings by Miles Evergood', *Art in Australia*, no. 49, April 1933, p. 17.

—— 'The Heysen loan exhibition', *Art in Australia*, no. 59, May 1935, p. 16.

—— 'Sea defence. Protecting trade routes. Navy's Policy. Manoeuvres as Test', *Sydney Morning Herald*, 14 February 1938, p. 8.

—— 'Gaps in our defences – Weapons and men lacking – Facts which must be faced', *Sydney Morning Herald*, 15 November 1938, p. 12.

—— 'France sees one spearhead of Britain's first million men under arms', *Brisbane Telegraph*, 14 October 1939, p. 2.

—— 'West Front. Effect of heavy rain. Problem of offensive', *Sydney Morning Herald*, 23 October 1939, p. 9.

—— 'Australian nurses work near front line', *Sydney Morning Herald*, 27 October 1939, p. 9.

—— 'Vivid rehearsal scenes: British front', *Brisbane Telegraph*, 3 November 1939, p. 4.

—— 'Experience in B.E.F. Chances missed. Few Australians in France', *Sydney Morning Herald*, 11 November 1939, p. 17.

—— 'Mechanised force test in deep mud', *Brisbane Telegraph*, 22 November 1939, p. 3.

—— 'Tank powerful and proved factor in war', *Brisbane Telegraph*, 30 November 1939, p. 6.

—— 'German bombers hammer Belgian defence line', *Sydney Morning Herald*, 14 May 1940, p. 9.

—— 'Troops pour into Belgium', *Sydney Morning Herald*, 15 May 1940, p. 13.

—— 'Big move to pocket B.E.F. in Belgium', *Brisbane Telegraph*, 21 May 1940, p. 1.

—— 'B.E.F. Moves closer to Belgium's coast', *Brisbane Telegraph*, 22 May 1940, p. 3.

—— 'Withdrawal in Belgium', *Sydney Morning Herald*, 23 May 1940, p. 9.

—— 'Strange story of how press correspondents were hustled to England', *Brisbane Telegraph*, 24 May 1940, p. 2.

—— 'NSW battalions chosen for assault', *Sydney Morning Herald*, 7 January 1941, p. 7.

—— 'Epic of withdrawal from Greece', *Sydney Morning Herald*, 5 May 1941, p. 10.

—— 'Comic-paper digger', *Sydney Morning Herald*, 24 June 1942, p. 6.

—— 'Re-making Australia's Army', *Sydney Morning Herald*, 6 August 1942, p. 4.

—— 'What AIF is thinking', *Sydney Morning Herald*, 26 August 1942, p. 6.

—— 'The real Australian soldier', *Australian News and Information Bureau*, New York, 1943. Reprinted from *The Infantry Journal*, June 1943.

—— *To Benghazi*, Australian War Memorial, Canberra, 1952.

—— *Greece, Crete and Syria*, Australian War Memorial, Canberra, 1953.

—— 'The Australian war history tradition', [typed manuscript of an address], ANZAAS Conference, Canberra, 12 January 1954, p. 2.

—— 'Sources of contemporary Australian military history', *Stand-To: Journal of the Australian Capital Territory Branch R.S.S.A.I.L.A.*, Canberra, Sept–Oct 1963a, pp. 8–12.

—— *The Final Campaigns*, Australian War Memorial, Canberra, 1963b.

—— 'Young Patterson and young Lawson', *Meanjin*, vol. 23, no. 4, 1964, pp. 403–413.

—— 'Looking back at two war histories', *Stand-To: Journal of the Australian Capital Territory Branch R.S.S.A.I.L.A*, Oct–Dec 1967, pp. 3–8.

—— *MacArthur as Military Commander*, Angus & Robertson, Sydney, 1969.

—— *The Six Years War: A Concise History of Australia in the 1939–45 War*, Australian War Memorial and Australian Government Publishing Service, Canberra, 1973.

Maclean, I, *A Guide to the Records of Gavin Long: being AWM 67, Official History, 1939–1945 War: Records of Gavin Long, General Editor*, Australian War Memorial, Canberra, 1993.

Maugham, B, *Tobruk and El Alamein*, Australian War Memorial, Canberra, 1966.

McCarthy, D, *South-West Pacific Area First Year – Kokoda to Wau*, Australian War Memorial, Canberra, 1959.

McKernan, M, *Here is Their Spirit: A History of the Australian War Memorial 1917–1990*, University of Queensland Press, St Lucia, 1991.

Mellor, D, *The Role of Science and Industry*, Australian War Memorial, Canberra, 1958.

Moffitt, I, *The U-Jack Society: An Experience of Being Australian*, Ure Smith, Sydney, 1972.

Moss, R, 'Gavin Merrick Long: Seeker of truth in war', *Canberra Times*, 11 October 1968, p. 2.

Murdoch, L, 'The day the empire died in shame', *Sydney Morning Herald*, 15 February 2012, <www.smh.com.au/national/the-day-the-empire-died-in-shame-20120214-1t462.html>, accessed 15 April 2022.

Odgers, G, *Air War Against Japan: 1939–1945*, Australian War Memorial, Canberra, 1957.

O'Neill, R, 'Australia in the Second World War', *Historical Studies*, vol. 16, no. 64, April 1975, pp. 456–461.

Paret, P, 'The history of war', *Daedalus*, vol. 100, no. 2, 1971, pp. 376–396, <www.jstor.org/stable/20024009>, accessed 3 September 2017.

Perry, W, 'Deaths of War Historians: Charles Bean and Gavin Long', *Victorian Historical Magazine*, vol. 39, November 1968, pp. 154–157.

Ramsey, A, 'A mateship that spoke volumes', *Sydney Morning Herald*, 22 April 2006.

Rees, P, *Bearing Witness*, Allen & Unwin, Sydney, 2015.

Semmler, C, (ed.) *The War Diaries of Kenneth Slessor: Official Australian Correspondent 1940–1944*, University of Queensland Press, Brisbane, 1985.

Souter, G, *Company of Heralds*, Melbourne University Press, Melbourne, 1981.

—— *Lion and Kangaroo: The Initiation of Australia 1901–1919*, Xoum Publishing, Sydney, 2017.

Stanley, P, 'The men who did the fighting are now all busy writing: Australian post-mortems on defeat in Malaya and Singapore, 1942–45', in B Farrell & S Hunter (eds), *Sixty Years On: The Fall of Singapore Revisited*, Eastern Universities Press, Singapore, 2002, pp. 290–312.

—— 'Gavin Long and history at the Australian War Memorial' in J Grey (ed.), *The Last Word? Essays on Official History in the United States and British Commonwealth*, Praeger, Westport, CN, 2003, pp. 105–116.

Steel, WA & Antill, JM, *The History of All Saints' College Bathurst 1873–1963*, Angus & Roberston, Sydney, 1964.

Stockings, C, *Bardia: Myth, Reality and the Heirs of Anzac*, UNSW Press, Sydney, 2009.

—— 'Deadly Pride and the Infamous Case of "Post 11"', *Australian Army Journal*, vol. 6, no. 2, 2009, pp. 117–137.

—— (ed.), *Zombie Myths of Australian Military History*, UNSW Press, Sydney, 2010.
—— (ed.), *Anzac's Dirty Dozen: 12 Myths of Australian Military History*, UNSW Press, 2012.
Stockings, C & Hancock, E, *Swastika Over the Acropolis: Re-interpreting the Nazi Invasion of Greece in World War II*, Leiden, Boston, 2013.
Sweeting, AJ, 'Long, Gavin Merrick (1901–1968)', Australian Dictionary of Biography, National Centre of Biography, Australian National University, Canberra, 2000.
—— 'Gavin Long, war historian: A memoir', *Canberra Historical Journal*, March 2007, pp. 2–7.
Tolstoy, L, *Sevastopol Sketches 1: Sevastopol in December 1854*, The Literature Network, n.d., <www.online-literature.com/tolstoy/sevastopol-sketches/1/>, accessed 20 July 2021.
Usher, J (ed.), *The Argus: Life & Death of a Newspaper*, Australian Scholarly Publishing, Melbourne, 2008.
Viney, Hannah, '"It was an Aussie ship which had escorted them home": the Royal Australian Navy in the evacuations of Greece and Crete, April–June, 1941', Australian War Memorial, Canberra, 2019, <www.awm.gov.au/sites/default/files/hannahss.pdf>, accessed 30 May 2023.
Wallis, N, *The Bathurstian*, Australian National Library, Canberra, 1937.
Ward, R, *A Nation for a Continent: The History of Australia 1901–1975*, Heinemann, Richmond, 1983.
Waterson, D, 'How to select a "proper" official historian', *Labour History*, no. 83, November 2002, pp. 191–194.
Wigmore, L, *The Japanese Thrust*, Australian War Memorial, Canberra, 1957.
—— 'Obituary – Gavin Long', *Historical Studies*, vol. 14, no. 53, October 1969, pp. 154–158.
Wilson, HC, *From Palings to Pavement: History of Foster*, Foster & District Historical Society, Foster, 1995.

**Archives and unpublished manuscripts**

Australian War Memorial registry files - Second series, c.1940–c.1968, AWM315.
Brown, G, *The 1942 Singapore Disaster: Assessing Recent Claims*, Department of the Parliamentary Library, 1993.
Keating, GM, *The Right Man for the Right Job: An Assessment of Lt. Gen. S.G. Savige as a Senior Commander* [honours thesis], University of New South Wales, Australian Defence Force Academy, 1995.
Official History, 1914–18 War: Records of CEW Bean, Official Historian, AWM38.
Official History, 1939–45 War: Records of Gavin Long, General Editor, AWM67.

# NOTES

**1 To crystallise the facts**

1 AWM67 [1/1], p. 3.

2 From a letter Clark wrote to Gavin Long's widow, Jocelyn, upon hearing of Gavin's death as recorded in L Wigmore, 'Obituary - Gavin Long', *Historical Studies,* vol. 14, no. 53, October 1969.

3 AJ Sweeting, 'Long, Gavin Merrick (1901–1968)', Australian Dictionary of Biography, National Centre of Biography, Australian National University, Canberra, 2000, accessed 16 June 2022.

4 J Hetherington, 'Australian writers in profile: Gavin Long', *The Age,* 12 November 1960.

5 The 22-volume history, published by the Australian War Memorial between 1952 and 1977, has been digitised and is available online, <www.awm.gov.au/collection/C1417143>.

6 R Moss, 'Seeker of truth in war', *Canberra Times,* 11 October 1968, p. 2.

7 M Koziol, 'Don't mention the war: Why Canberra suppresses the story of East Timor', *Sydney Morning Herald,* 24 November 2019.

8 In the months following the Second World War, when approving Long's plan for the official history, the War Cabinet agreed that 'the exercise of censorship by the Government is to be limited to the prevention of disclosure of technical secrets of the three Services which it is necessary to preserve in the post-war period'. G Long, *To Benghazi,* Australian War Memorial, Canberra, 1952, p. xi.

9 G Long, 'The australian war history tradition', [typed manuscript of an address], ANZAAS Conference, Canberra, 12 January 1954, p. 2. The typed manuscript can be found in AWM67 [9/4]. Long's address was reprinted in the Canberra Historical Journal (November 1954) and *Stand-To: Journal of the Australian Capital Territory Branch R.S.S.A.I.L.A.* (Mar–Apr 1955).

10 P Paret, 'The history of war', *Daedalus,* vol. 100, no. 2, 1971, pp. 376–396, <www.jstor.org/stable/20024009>, accessed 3 September, 2017.

11 Paret 1971, p. 382.

12 Long 1954, p. 13.

13 Long 1954.

14 J Hetherington, *Forty-Two Faces: Profiles of Living Australian Writers,* FW Cheshire, Melbourne, 1962, p. 58.

15 Long 1954, p. 13.

16 Long 1954, p. 3.

17 CEW Bean, 'Our war history', *Bulletin,* 27 May 1942, p. 2.

18 P Rees, *Bearing Witness,* Allen & Unwin, Sydney, 2015, p. 113.

19 Bean, 'Our war history'.

20 G Long, 'Looking back at two war histories', *Stand-To: Journal of the Australian Capital Territory Branch R.S.S.A.I.L.A.,* Oct–Dec 1967, p. 4.

21 Published by the Australian War Memorial and now available digitally: <www.awm.gov.au/collection/C1416531>. Bean's official history comprises roughly 10 000 pages, 4 million words, 2250 maps and sketches, and 1500 illustrations.

22 Rees 2015, p. 398.

23 CEW Bean, 'Sidelights of the war on Australian character', *Royal Australian Historical Society Journal,* vol. 13 pt. 4, 1927, p. 211.
24 AWM38 3DRL 6673/498, 23 June 1930.
25 AWM38 3DRL 6673/498, 30 June 1930.
26 AWM38 3DRL 6673/498, 2 Nov 1938.
27 Bean, 'Our war history'.

**2 My dear Long**

1 G Hermon Gill, 'War historian Gavin Long dead', *The Age*, 11 October, 1968, p. 6.
2 G Souter, *Lion and Kangaroo: The Initiation of Australia*, Xoum Publishing, Sydney, 2017, p. 10.
3 Souter 2017, p. 97.
4 Souter 2017, p. 134.
5 CEW Bean, *Flagships Three*, Hodder & Stoughton, London, 1916, p. 216.
6 W Johnson, *The Right Reverend George Merrick Long, Lord Bishop of Bathurst 1911–1928, Lord Bishop of Newcastle 1928–1930: A Memoir*, St John's College Press, Morpeth, 1930, p. 21.
7 'The morality of imperialism', *The Age*, 5 August 1899, p. 9; 'The morality of imperialism', *Argus*, 5 August 1899, p. 9; 'The morality of imperialism, *Australasian*, 12 August 1899, p. 33.
8 Johnson 1930, p. 29.
9 Johnson 1930, p. 27.
10 Wallis's reflections appear in the 1937 edition of *The Bathurstian* held in the Australian National Library on microfilm.
11 WA Steel & JM Antill, *The History of All Saints' College Bathurst 1873–1963*, Angus & Robertson, Sydney, 1964.
12 Long family papers.
13 Long family papers.
14 For CEW Bean's detailed account of George Long's monumental efforts to establish the AIF Education Scheme in 1918–1919, see the *Official History of Australia in the War of 1914–1918, Vol. VI – The Australian Imperial Force in France during the Allied Offensive, 1918*, The Australian War Memorial, 1942, pp. 1062–1072.
15 Long family papers.
16 Long family papers.
17 Long family papers.
18 *Sydney Morning Herald*, 8 May 1919, p. 8.
19 J Hetherington, *Forty-Two Faces: Profiles of Living Australian Writers*, FW Cheshire, Melbourne, 1962, p. 56.

**3 Newspaperman, arts critic and defence commentator**

1 G Souter, *Company of Heralds*, Melbourne University Press, Melbourne, 1981, p. 181.
2 Long family papers.
3 J Hetherington, 'Australian writers in profile: Gavin Long', *The Age*, 12 November 1960.
4 Long family papers.
5 G Long, 'Record-breaking in the fifties: Prodigious feats of the Flying Pieman', *Argus*, 27 September 1930, p. 2.
6 T Merrick, 'Some London theatres', *The Triad: A Journal Devoted To Literacy, Pictorial, Musical and Dramatic Art*, August 1925, p. 33.

7 B Griffen-Foley (ed.), *A Companion to the Australian Media*, Australian Scholarly Publishing, Kew, 2014.
8 G Long, 'A layman's complaint', *Art in Australia*, no. 42, February 1932, pp. 20–22.
9 G Long, 'Some paintings by Miles Evergood', *Art in Australia*, no. 49, April 1933, p. 17.
10 Long family papers.
11 G Long, 'Young Paterson and young Lawson', *Meanjin*, vol. 23, no. 4, 1964, p. 403.
12 P Rees, *Bearing Witness*, Allen & Unwin, Sydney, 2015, p. 401.
13 G Souter, *Lion and Kangaroo: The Initiation of Australia*, Xoum Publishing, Sydney, 2017 pp. 127–128.
14 CEW Bean, 'Sidelights of the war on Australian', *Journal of the Royal Australian Historical Society*, vol. 13, pt. 4, 1927, p. 211.
15 G Long, 'The Comic-paper digger', *Sydney Morning Herald*, 24 June 1942, p. 6.
16 AWM67 [13/1].
17 AWM67 [13/1].
18 Long family papers.
19 B Juddery, 'War expert drops hint', *Canberra Times*, 24 April 1968, p. 18.
20 G Long, 'Sea defence. Protecting trade routes. Navy's policy. Manoeuvres as test', *Sydney Morning Herald*, 14 February 1938, p. 8.
21 G Long, 'Gaps in our defences – Weapons and men lacking – Facts which must be faced', *Sydney Morning Herald*, 15 November 1938, p. 12.

**4 Our own correspondent**

1 G Long, 'Withdrawal in Belgium', *Sydney Morning Herald*, 23 May 1940, p. 9.
2 AWM38 3DRL 6673/498.
3 Long family papers.
4 Many of the anecdotes relating to the experiences of the Longs in London during 1939 are extracted from Jocelyn's very detailed personal daily diary in the Long family papers.
5 AWM67 [13/14 A–F].
6 Long family papers.
7 Long family papers.
8 G Souter, *Company of Heralds*, Melbourne University Press, Melbourne, 1981, p. 208.
9 G Long, 'Australian nurses work near front line', *Sydney Morning Herald*, 27 October 1939, p. 9.
10 G Long, 'France sees one spearhead of Britain's first million men under arms', *Brisbane Telegraph*, 14 October 1939, p. 2.
11 G Long, 'West Front. Effect of heavy rain. Problem of offensive', *Sydney Morning Herald*, 23 October, 1939, p. 9.
12 G Long, 'Vivid rehearsal scenes: British Front', *Brisbane Telegraph*, 3 November 1939, p. 4.
13 G Long, 'Experience in B.E.F. Chances missed. Few Australians in France', *Sydney Morning Herald*, 11 November 1939, p. 17.
14 G Long, 'Mechanised force test in deep mud', *Brisbane Telegraph*, 22 November 1939, p. 3.
15 G Long, 'Tank powerful and proved factor in war', *Brisbane Telegraph*, 30 November 1939, p. 6.
16 C Semmler, *The War Diaries of Kenneth Slessor*, University of Queensland Press, Brisbane, 1985, p. xx.
17 Souter 1981, p. 206; Lower was a notoriously inebriate humorist and novelist.

**5 A fairly strenuous time**

1 B Juddery, 'War expert drops hint', *Canberra Times,* 24 April 1968, p. 18.
2 Long family papers.
3 G Long, 'Troops pour into Belgium', *Sydney Morning Herald,* 15 May 1940, p. 13.
4 Long, 'Troops Pour Into Belgium'.
5 G Long, 'German bombers hammer Belgian defence line', *Sydney Morning Herald,* 14 May 1940, p. 9.
6 G Long, 'Strange story of how press correspondents were hustled to England', *Brisbane Telegraph,* 24 May 1940, p. 2.
7 Long, 'Strange Story of How Press Correspondents Were Hustled to England'.
8 G Long, 'Big move to pocket B.E.F. in Belgium', *Brisbane Telegraph,* 21 May 1940, p. 1.
9 G Long, 'B.E.F. moves closer to Belgium's coast', *Brisbane Telegraph*, 22 May 1940, p. 3.
10 Long family papers.
11 Long family papers.
12 Souter 1981, p. 181.
13 Long family papers.
14 Long family papers.
15 Long family papers.
16 Long family papers.
17 Long family papers.
18 E Gorman, 'The glory that is Greece', *Brisbane Truth*, 26 August 1942, p. 6.
19 Long family papers.
20 Long family papers.
21 G Long, 'Epic of withdrawal from Greece, *Sydney Morning Herald*, 5 May 1941, p. 10.
22 AWM67 [1/3], pp. 24–27.
23 AWM67 [1/8], p. 43.
24 G Long, 'Re-making Australia's Army', *Sydney Morning Herald*, 6 August 1942, p. 4.
25 AWM67 [1/9], p.13.
26 AWM67 [1/9], p. 14.
27 G Long, 'What AIF is thinking' *Sydney Morning Herald*, 26 August 1942, p. 6.
28 AWM67 [1/9], p. 17.

**6 Before it is too late**

1 CEW Bean, 'Our war history', *Bulletin*, 27 May 1942, p. 2.
2 C Semmler, *The War Diaries of Kenneth Slessor*, University of Queensland Press, Brisbane, 1985, p. 327. Slessor wrote this while in Cairo on 5 December 1941.
3 P Rees, *Bearing Witness*, Allen & Unwin, Sydney, 2015, p 471.
4 Rees 2015, p. 471–472.
5 Rees 2015, p. 472.
6 AWM67 [9/4].
7 AWM67 [9/4].
8 J Hetherington, 'Australian writers in profile: Gavin Long', *The Age*, 12 November 1960.
9 AWM67 [1/9], p. 78f.
10 G Long, *To Benghazi*, Australian War Memorial, Canberra, 1952, p. xi.
11 Long 1952, p. xi.
12 AWM67 [9/1].
13 Gavin Long's diaries are preserved in the Australian War Memorial collection – AWM67 [1/1-14]. In them, Long recorded various aspects of his work as general editor of *Australia in the War of 1939–1945*.

14 While Long uses the term 'Official History' in his diary, no decision had yet been taken on the name of the work.
15 Long 1952, p. x.
16 L Wigmore, *The Japanese Thrust*, Australian War Memorial, Canberra, 1957, p. xii.
17 AWM67 [1/1], p. 64.
18 AWM67 [1/4], p. 66.
19 AWM67 [1/2], pp. 13–14.
20 AWM67 [1/2], pp. 13–14.
21 The annual Christmas book, *Khaki and Green: With the Australian Army at Home and Overseas*, was published by the Australian War Memorial.
22 AWM67 [1/3], p. 20.
23 AWM67 [1/1], p. 81.
24 AWM67 [1/2], p. 43.
25 AWM67 [1/1], p. 40. Evatt's criticism seems to have been ill-informed. He believed, for example, that Bean had failed to note the letter of General Birdwood to the troops urging them to vote in favour of conscription. After mentioning this supposed oversight to him, Bean objected that the letter from Birdwood had been included.
26 AWM67 [1/1], pp. 30–31.
27 AWM67 [1/1], p. 35.
28 AWM67 [1/3], pp. 50–51.
29 AWM67 [1/1], p. 69.
30 AWM67 [1/11], p. 34.
31 AWM67 [1/2], pp. 46–48.
32 AWM67 [1/5], p. 35.
33 Hetherington, 'Australian writers in profile: Gavin Long'.

**7 A true and faithful record**

1 AWM67 [1/7], p. 29.
2 AWM67 [9/1].
3 AWM67 [1/1], p. 2.
4 AWM67 [1/1], p. 2.
5 AWM67 [1/2], pp. 7–9.
6 AWM67 [1/2], p. 29.
7 AWM67 [1/2], p. 82.
8 AWM67 [4/17], pp. 8–11.
9 AWM67 [4/21].
10 AJ Sweeting, 'Gavin Long, war historian: a memoir', *Canberra Historical Journal*, March 2007, pp. 3–5.
11 AWM67 [1/4], p. 74.
12 Long family papers.
13 L Tolstoy, *Sevastopol Sketches 1: Sevastopol in December 1854*, The Literature Network, n.d., <www.online-literature.com/tolstoy/sevastopol-sketches/1/>, accessed 20 July 2021.
14 G Long, *To Benghazi*, Australian War Memorial, Canberra, 1952, p. 164.
15 G Long, 'The Australian War History Tradition', [typed manuscript of an address], ANZAAS Conference, Canberra, 12 January 1954, p. 2.
16 G Long, *Greece, Crete and Syria*, Australian War Memorial, 1953, p. 311.
17 G Long, 'Looking back at two war histories', *Stand-To: Journal of the Australian Capital Territory Branch R.S.S.A.I.L.A*, Oct–Dec 1967, p. 6.

18 Long 1952, p. xi.
19 AWM38 3DRL 6673/463.

**8 Assembling the narratives**

1 AJ Sweeting, 'Long, Gavin Merrick (1901–1968)', Australian Dictionary of Biography, National Centre of Biography, Australian National University, Canberra, 2000, accessed 16 June 2022.
2 G Long, 'The Australian War History Tradition', [typed manuscript of an address], ANZAAS Conference, Canberra, 12 January 1954, p. 6.
3 G Long, *The Final Campaigns*, Australian War Memorial, Canberra, 1963b, p. xvi.
4 J Herington, *Air War Against Germany and Italy 1939–1943*, Australian War Memorial, Canberra, 1954, p. xv.
5 D Mellor, *The Role of Science and Industry*, Australian War Memorial, Canberra, 1958, p. ix.
6 B Maugham, *Tobruk and El Alamein*, Australian War Memorial, Canberra, 1966, p. xv.
7 D Gillison, *Royal Australian Air Force, 1939–1942*, Australian War Memorial, Canberra, 1962, p. xii.
8 P Hasluck, *The Government and the People, 1939–1941*, Australian War Memorial, Canberra, [1952]1965, p. xii.
9 AWM67 [1/4], p. 75.
10 AWM67 [4/1], p. 1.
11 L Wigmore, *The Japanese Thrust*, Australian War Memorial, Canberra, 1957, p. xi.
12 AWM67 [4/13], p. 24.
13 AWM67 [1/13], p. 11.
14 AJ Sweeting, 'Gavin Long, war historian: a memoir', *Canberra Historical Journal*, March 2007, p. 3.
15 S Jamieson, 'Gavin Long – An appreciation', *The Bathurstian: The Magazine of All Saints' College Bathurst*, All Saints' College, Bathurst, 1968.
16 AWM67 [13/7], p. 3.
17 AWM67 [1/10], p. 58.
18 AWM67 [1/10], pp. 28–29.
19 AWM67 [1/10].
20 AWM67 [13/1].
21 G Long, 'Sources of contemporary Australian military history', *Stand-To: Journal of the Australian Capital Territory Branch R.S.S.A.I.L.A.*, Canberra, Sept–Oct 1963a, pp. 8–12.
22 Long 1963a, p. 10.
23 Long 1963a, p. 10.
24 AWM67 [1/6], p. 34.
25 AWM67 [13/1].
26 Wigmore, *The Japanese Thrust*, p. xii.
27 AWM67 [1/3], p. 41.
28 AWM67 [1/12], p. 74.

**9 His devoted staff**

1 G Hermon Gill, 'War historian Gavin Long dead', *The Age*, 11 October, 1968, p. 6.
2 AWM67 [1/7], p. 36.
3 G Long, *The Six Years War: A Concise History of Australia in the 1939–45 War*, Australian War Memorial, Canberra, 1973, p. xiii.

4 AJ Sweeting, *Gavin Merrick Long OBE – War historian and noble Australian,* [typed manuscript of an address given to AWM Guides], c. late 1970s, Long family papers.
5 AWM67 [1/12], p. 29.

## 10 The generation that belongs to this war

1 G Hermon Gill, *Royal Australian Navy, 1942–1945*, Australian War Memorial, Canberra, 1968, p. xiv.
2 AWM67 [1/6], p. 48.
3 AWM67 [1/3], p. 6.
4 AWM67 [1/4], pp. 66–67.
5 AWM67 [3/374], pt. 1.
6 AWM67 [1/9], p. 83.
7 AWM67 [1/2], p. 18.
8 AWM67 [1/4], p. 66.
9 AWM67 [1/12], p. 9.
10 AWM67 [1/12], p. 66.
11 AWM67 [1/12], p. 78.
12 Long family papers.
13 D McCarthy, *South-West Pacific Area First Year – Kokoda to Wau*, Australian War Memorial, Canberra, 1959, p. 307.
14 D Dexter, *The New Guinea Offensives*, Australian War Memorial, Canberra, 1961, p. xvi.
15 *RAAF News*, December 1965.
16 G Odgers, *Air War Against Japan: 1939–1945*, Australian War Memorial, Canberra, 1957.
17 L Wigmore, 'Obituary: Two war historians', *Historical Studies*, University of Melbourne, vol. 14, no. 53, October 1969, p. 156.
18 Long family papers.
19 W Perry, 'Deaths of war historians: Charles Bean and Gavin Long', *The Victorian Historical Magazine*, Royal Historical Society of Victoria, vol. 39, issue 154, November 1968, p. 156.

## 11 Criticisms of Gavin Long and the official history

1 R O'Neill, 'Australia in the Second World War', *Historical Studi*es, vol. 16, no. 64, April 1975, p. 459.
2 P Elphick, *Singapore: The Pregnable Fortress: A Study in Deception, Discord and Desertion*, Hodder & Stoughton, London, 1995, p. 363.
3 For a detailed account of the important history published in December 1954 by Lieutenant Colonel Charles 'Gus' Kappe and glossed over by both the British and Australian official historians, see P Stanley, 'The Men who did the fighting are now all busy writing: Australian post-mortems in Malaya and Singapore, 1942–1945' in Farrell & Hunter (eds), *Sixty Years On: The Fall of Singapore Revisited*, Eastern Universities Press, Singapore, 2002, pp. 290–312.
4 Elphick 1995, p. 338.
5 L Murdoch, 'The day the empire died in shame', *Sydney Morning Herald*, 15 February 2012, <www.smh.com.au/national/the-day-the-empire-died-in-shame-20120214-1t462.html>, accessed 15 April 2022.
6 Stanley in Farrell & Hunter 2003, p. 307.

7 C Stockings, *Bardia: Myth, Reality and the Heirs of Anzac*, UNSW Press, Sydney, 2009, p. 295.
8 Stockings 2009, p. 296.
9 For a critique of Craig Stockings' *Bardia: Myth, Reality and the Heirs of Anzac*, see D Kerr, 'Bardia: Myth, reality and the heirs of ANZAC' in *Australian Army Journal*, vol. 7, no. 2, 2010, pp. 139–144. Kerr asserts that Stockings brushes over morale as a factor and downplays the importance of the high expectations Australian soldiers felt keen to live up to (that of the AIF) and that the Anzac myth/legend is not all there is to that legend. If seen as an ideal to aim for, a soldier/an army may well perform better.
10 G Long, 'NSW battalions chosen for assault', *Sydney Morning Herald*, 7 January 1941, p. 7.
11 Stockings 2009, p. 292.
12 Stockings 2009, p. 295.
13 Stockings 2009, p. 295.
14 Stockings 2009, p. 297.
15 Undated manuscript about the scheme and writers of the official history project, AWM67 [13/07], p. 8.
16 J Ross, as quoted in Stockings 2009, p. 301.
17 G Long, *To Benghazi*, Australian War Memorial, Canberra, 1952, pp. 203–206.
18 Long 1952, p. 205.
19 However, military historian David Horner has argued consistently that the New Guinea and Bougainville offensives were 'probably necessary'.
20 P Charlton, *The Unnecessary War: Island Campaigns of the South-West Pacific 1944–1945*, Macmillan, Melbourne, 1983, p. 170.
21 G Long, *The Final Campaigns*, Australian War Memorial, Canberra, 1963b, p. 386.
22 Long 1963, p. 327.
23 Long 1963, p. 342.
24 Long 1963, p. xvi.
25 O'Neill 1975, p. 456.

**Epilogue: His final campaigns**

1 B Juddery, 'War expert drops hint', *Canberra Times*, 24 April, 1968, p. 18.
2 AWM collection, accession number F10131.
3 M Clark, 'Honour, duty and errors', *Canberra Times*, 16 August, 1969, p. 13.
4 R O'Neill, 'Australia in the Second World War', *Historical Studies*, vol. 16, no. 64, April 1975, pp. 456–461.
5 O'Neill 1975, p. 460.
6 Sweeting 2007, p. 6.
7 Sweeting 2007, p. 7.
8 AWM563/003/032.
9 AWM232/003/026.
10 O'Neill 1975, p. 456.

# INDEX